THE
TERRITORY
OF MEN

VILLARD  NEW YORK

THE
TERRITORY
OF MEN

A MEMOIR

Joelle Fraser

Earlier versions of two chapters were published in slightly different form:
"Release" as "Riot" in *Fourth Genre*, Winter 2000; and "Karyn's Story" as
"Karyn's Murder" in *Zyzzyva*, Fall 1998.

Library of Congress Cataloging-in-Publication Data is available.
ISBN: 0-375-50437-0

Villard Books website address: www.villard.com
Printed in the United States of America on acid-free paper
9 8 7 6 5 4 3 2
First Edition   *4997*

Book design by Victoria Wong

To my mother and father

And to my brothers, Dace and Ken,
who journeyed with me

Acknowledgments

I would like to thank my agent, Jandy Nelson, for her boundless support and friendship, and my editor, Susanna Porter, for her wisdom and her fine attention to both the line and the story. The MacDowell Colony I thank for their generous support. For their support, Howard Junker, Patricia Foster, and David Hamilton. For their early guidance and teaching, I am truly grateful to Dana Elder and Paul Diehl. For believing in me, many thanks to Roy Parvin and Sherman Alexie. The faith and encouragement of friends and family during the writing of this book continue to amaze me: Mahalo to Mark, Kaui, Melissa, Eliza, Celia, Tina, and Richelle. Kathy, my aunt, was always ready to listen to portions of the book over the phone, and she offered invaluable insight and encouragement.

And to Joe, for his faith in me that never wavered; he will always have my deepest appreciation and respect.

Finally, it is with love that I acknowledge my mother's brave support of this book. Her kindness and generosity will never cease to inspire me.

Contents

THE
TERRITORY
OF MEN

Summertime

MOTHER'S DAY, 1966

W atch us as we barrel across that bright bridge toward San Francisco, the gray waves of the ocean seething and crashing below. It's a warm May day, the windows are wide open, and my mother's black hair flies wildly around her sweating face.

We're late for the hospital, but traffic is light—and this is a party, after all, one that began in the morning and lasted all night and hasn't stopped for years. In the backseat, my father sits between two friends, smoking a cigarette, lips stained dark from gin and grape juice. He grins at my mother in front, tells her to hold on. He says wouldn't it be a great story if they had a baby on the Golden Gate Bridge.

The Mamas and the Papas' "California Dreamin' " comes on the radio, and everyone sings, the words swept up by scarves of fog and spread over the sea. They're drunk, all of them, all but my mother, who leans back to ease the pain, belly swollen, legs braced because it's almost time and I'm pushing to get out.

That summer my mother's twenty-four and broke, living in a small flat in Sausalito with an infant, and my father's away somewhere trying to earn money. He's lost jobs, as a shoe salesman, as a ranger in Muir Woods—he was let go for not keeping the latrines clean enough. This last job, at a landscaping company, they fired him for pulling out the jasmine instead of the weeds. He's been away from home for weeks.

She reads my father's letter, which says he's lost his fourth job, and it's his fourth job in half a year. Life is much harder now with a baby, and she suspects that it will not ease up soon, or ever. She remembers those wonderful evenings after they were first married, living here in Sausalito, drinking Red Mountain wine at three dollars a gallon, feet dangling over the water as the fog lifted and the small boats floated by on the bay, with San Francisco's lights beyond. She thinks of the late nights at *Contact,* the art magazine they worked at in the city, and the concerts at the Fillmore. She has all the memories of the year before, in New York, when he worked at *Look* and she at *Mademoiselle.* In New York, the party began Wednesday and ended late Monday night: their home was an open invitation to visit anytime but Tuesday. They made jokes about their lifestyle, how it was like the title from Hemingway's book *A Moveable Feast.* Almost every night they drank, and in the morning woke to friends passed out on their floor.

They were both dreamers, but my mother had a practical side, and it was mostly this concern for the future and for a sense of security that came between them. When they argued, it was about money, which fell through the cracks of their lives, emptied on booze and parties and books. But they had loved each other while it was just the two of them, and that was all that really mattered.

Then she got pregnant with me and they headed back west.

My mother tries not to think about the way her life has turned, how somewhere along the way the wheel jerked and took a hard left onto a road she didn't want to go down or wasn't ready for. The pregnancy had not been planned; it was a ridiculous thing—a baby!— when they were so poor, and so full of dreams of being writers, and there was this sense of promise that was inspired partly by their youth, but also by something beyond them, a firey optimism that surrounded them in California in the sixties. My mother has always felt there is a purpose for her, as if she has been selected to do something special, the exact nature of which hasn't yet been revealed. And how would she fulfill that destiny now, with a baby and its many, constant needs? One day she passes the one window with a view of the bay, just a slice, a strip of gray-blue above the roof next door. In the distance, the boat masts at the harbor look like white sticks. She checks on me, and my dependence both frightens and emboldens her. My needs are deceptively simple, and she suspects she makes mistakes no matter how hard she tries. She doesn't wrap me in blankets, as she saw her mother do with her younger siblings, but leaves me open to the air, which I try to grab, my legs and arms springy, reaching for something to hold on to. She thinks this is best, that I am free, unbound, and she doesn't understand my agitation. She returns to the kitchen and pours a glass of wine, decides that she will carry me along with her the way she carries her books and belongings, and that I will have to adapt to the choices she makes. As if I know what is expected, I travel well, rarely cry. I learn to be quiet.

At night she misses my father, his presence beside her in bed, the way he lights his cigarette, his pet names that lift her from her deepest frustration. Something is missing—there is a void, a sense of waiting, of abandonment. Her aloneness feels wrong; his absence depresses her. One evening, looking over the courtyard below and the bay beyond, my mother throws a glass of red wine against the wall. The wine runs like pink watercolor, and she fills another glass and throws that one, too. She does that until the bottle is gone and all the glasses are broken but one.

Sometimes the fog lifts and it's warm, and my mother forgets about the cold nights and her loneliness and how she will find groceries for the week. She reads with the sleeping cats for company; carries me to the Lighthouse coffee shop on clear mornings. Sometimes the woman behind the counter gives her a free coffee or a Danish. In the afternoons my mother sits with me in the small courtyard, among the pots of marigolds and geraniums that flourish in the heat and fog.

In her journal she writes about the beauty of this town by the bay. Sausalito is unspoiled—there is still beachfront that has not been developed, and groves of willow trees stand where condominiums will come later. Many of the roads she walks on are not even paved; they're just dirt, pocked with potholes that fill with rainwater in winter. Below our apartment, a Frenchwoman lives with her husband, who plays the violin in the evenings. The woman prepares lovely noon meals: braised snails, a French broth, homemade bread. My mother smells this through the open window as she carries me up the wooden stairs to our apartment.

Weeks later my father sends for us—we're moving to the island of Kauai, where we'll be safe from worry about money and jobs and having enough to eat. Hawaii is my father's home; his mother, who lives in Honolulu, has come up with just enough money and a lead on a job in construction, a new hotel. We move into a small cottage in Anahola, far out in the country, steps from the ocean. Even though we have little money and the house has no electricity, no phone, no radio, my mother is hopeful. She spends her days swimming with me in shallow waves, napping in the hot afternoons. She eats mangoes and oranges from the trees in back. The nearest town, Lihue, is an hour's drive; thus the beach, though beautiful, is so remote that people rarely come. Most nights my mother's are the only footprints that remain on the sand. She wears bright muumuus, the billowing floor-length dresses the missionaries brought to drape over Hawaiian women. At first she worries that she looks matronly, but my father assures her the dresses are alluring for what they hide, and hint at.

When he gets home from work, sometimes he takes me for a walk on the beach, or along the red dirt road that runs along the cane fields, carrying me like a book under his arm, singing to me.

At night the two of them drink wine on the lanai and listen to the rustle of palm trees, the *cluckcluck* of geckos, the waves and light at sunset like a dance performed each day. The most important piece of my parents' story is that they were very deeply in love. This love was so strong, so natural, that I wonder if either found such a strange mixture of passion and contentment again.

My mother writes in her journal:

February 11, 1967

Harriet our landlady brought papayas, oranges and a grass doll for Joelle. We have a beautiful garden all around. Orange trees in back, chickens, and 10ft high poinsettias. It rained all day. Ken started novel. Joelle to be a beautiful child, Kenneth a writer and myself a person again. Sounds like I have the easy job but remnants of New York, the moves of '66, the baby have combined to make the task "formidable."

A time to begin now.

My father loses his job and finds another at the golf course, for less pay. Now and then they go to town and drink cocktails in the hotel bar, overlooking the harbor. A Hawaiian woman watches me when they're gone. She tells my mother the Hawaiian spirits love children and that I will be safe. She wears a necklace of dog teeth.

When he's not working, my father tries to write, but he's frustrated by the slow progress. In just a few months my mother will leave, return to the mainland with me.

February 21

A really beautiful day for us. As of the moment we have $4 to our name, but it never seems to bother Ken and I'm beginning to feel the same, too. Yesterday we drove to a natural slide and pool, slick with moss, ½ mile walk in. Ken slid first and then I finally did. Joelle was put in a little pool. She doesn't mind the cool water at all. At home, he attempted writing. Quit. I told him he had to work harder. He was quiet and then said he would try it my way. So this morning up at breakfast and writing til noon or when Joelle awakes and then lunch, maybe a swim, a nap and writing from 3 to 5 or 6. He's quiet in there now.

My father, overwhelmed, leaves for days at a time, borrows money from his boss, from his mother, often flying to Oahu to see his old high school friends in Honolulu, and my mother's loneliness and isolation overwhelm her. With so much time on her hands, she reads her old textbooks on physics and psychology, becomes absorbed in them.

April 10

A girl has loaned us a typewriter. Ken seems intent on it, although I think he writes in longhand. I worry about his job, 10 hours a day at the golf course. They are long, boring hours. If he doesn't get into a book I cannot picture him doing this for long. Such a waste but if he can write, it will be all right.

At night there are no lights, and on moonless nights the ocean is black. She is terrified of the giant cane rats that scrabble on the roof for mangoes fallen from the trees. My father tells her he can't write his novel. He drinks steadily. As I read the journal I'm afraid, because I know what will happen—it's like reading a book and knowing the end: it's going to be a heartbreaker. I want to rewrite her words. I want to go back and tell her, *Don't go, keep trying.*

May 1

The writing is his problem to solve. I will simply make him happy as I haven't been doing lately and perhaps things will fall into place. He doesn't fit. He just doesn't. He will never have one job, maybe a variety of them with writing on the side. This year will tell a lot. Writing, writing, I know this is it. I'm just afraid he will come home one night with that look and we'll be off again. Vagabonds. We need a rest. . . . Joelle has 7 teeth, lighter blond hair and a love for books . . .

In June, just after my first birthday, my mother packs her things and mine. She and my father, not trusting each other to hug, afraid they won't let go, simply shake hands outside the Kauai Surf Hotel, while the wind gusts from Nawiliwili Harbor behind them.

My mother takes me to her parents in Oregon and returns alone to Sausalito to find work. For three months I stay with my grandparents and my aunt Barbara, a teenager. Barbara, with her curly hair and soft laugh, holds me and sings to me, and when I close my eyes, she sounds like my mother. Every night before I sleep, they show me my mother's picture, and sometimes my father's, holding the photo close to my face so I can touch it.

When she comes back for me that September, I know her; though it has been a summer, I know my mother, and I put my arms around her, bury my head in the curve of her warm neck, and hold her with all my small strength. Surprised, she holds out her arms to her sides—"Look, Ma, no arms"—and everyone laughs at the baby clinging to her like a little monkey. For a long time she can't get free, I won't let go.

1969: Joelle, age three

Kaleidoscope

From fragments I put together a story. I see myself in photos, hear myself in my mother's stories. I know that I spent my childhood in a place of color and music, full of people, and there was constant change. And I know some details. That I slept in a drawer as a baby. That we were always very poor. I wore satin and velvet collected from boxes we found in the street. These fragments intersect with my own memories, which are of the senses—the smell of eucalyptus, the feel of grass under my bare feet, the sounds of guitar and singing. When I think of my childhood, it is like looking into a kaleidoscope: shifting, colorful, exciting. But unlike the toy, these images and memories and stories never rest, never settle into a shape.

For years my story was inseparable from my mother's. She took me to Sausalito, to the upstairs apartment on Easterby Street, with its twin windows overlooking the bay. This was where my mother and I began our life without my father. A long, narrow staircase rose to our door, and it was a labored climb for me—I had to thrust my knee over the wooden edge, lifting my belly, step by step. We must have lived there almost two years, until I turned four.

Sometimes, late at night after concerts at the Fillmore in San

Francisco, my mother's younger sister Kathy and her friends stopped by on their way home to the houseboats. They came dressed in long coats and feathers and dangling jewelry. I remember the blur of voices, high leather boots clicking on the floor. They snorted cocaine from long white ribbons on the kitchen table.

I never interrupted. I didn't like to be the center of things, because I never knew quite what to expect, and also because there was always someone new who made me feel shy. I'd whisper in my mother's ear if I had a question, or if something caught my eye that I wanted to play with.

We never knew when people would come by; many of them were drifting from place to place. They'd visit with us for an afternoon or a day or two, then leave notes with us for other friends, messages to pass on.

My mother found a job at a TV station in the city. While she worked, I stayed with Kathy, who lived close by in a houseboat at the Gate 5 marina. On my mother's days off, we often took long walks. She had very little money, so these walks had a purpose: we gathered things. We found clothes in the Goodwill box alongside Gate 5, where people left things they no longer wanted. We cut up fabric for tablecloths and napkins, and we helped ourselves, my mother holding up pants and shirts against her body, twirling as I laughed.

We were gypsies, dressed in shawls and hats and bright beads, strands of puka shells. Along the way we picked flowers for the vase on the windowsill, blue flax and roses and fennel, which I chewed on because I loved the licorice taste—it was the only sort of candy I could get.

Someone gave me a red velvet vest, and I wore it all the time. Dozens of tiny circular mirrors were sewn into it. It was Indian, ornate and fancy, like a costume. People stooped down to touch it, to look at their tiny reflections.

My mother was beautiful. She never wore makeup; she didn't need it anyway. In Portland, where she had modeled swimsuits for

Jantzen, and where she was chosen to be Rose Festival Princess at Jefferson High School, people described her beauty as "classic." She had blue eyes and black hair, hair strong as rope you could grab with two fists. Her beauty was an accident, a fact she had to accommodate in her life, like the weather—a thing that was part of her life but not central to it.

It is difficult to have a beautiful mother. People want to be with her, she attracts men constantly. She is like a fire that draws them to her. She makes them believe she could do anything for them, with them. The desire I felt for her was different, though it was just as physical. I wanted her presence, her nearness—I wanted her to stand beside me, to hold me. I had to learn to share, to wait my turn.

In all my memories of San Francisco and Sausalito, it is summer. There must have been winter, months of rain, but I don't remember. The closest I come to a feeling of cold is the presence of swirling fog, hovering always at the edge of my childhood.

Michael came to live with us. My mother met him at her job, where he wrote sales copy at a desk across from hers. He was with us for a year—though he would come in and out of our lives until I was much older, about eight or nine, and by that time I loved him like a father. In that first year, he helped her forget about my father in Hawaii, whom she missed deeply and still wrote letters to. Michael was tall, and his hair was blond and thick like my father's, and he loved me. At night he rocked me and read to me.

Sometimes when he was napping, I'd see my mother prop herself on her elbow and watch his face, his breathing. At night we all slept together. I lay at the foot of the bed in my own blanket. She wrote in her journal that she thought of Michael as a dance. She said they forgot about eating, and he told her she was beautiful twenty times a day. She wrote that he was less demanding than my father, who had edited her thoughts and tastes.

I began to notice how important men were to her, how they made her happy, alive. She would be nervous if Michael was late. Her body would straighten; she'd smooth back her hair. These were things she did for Michael, and for my father before him. The air changed, became taut. When she finally saw him through the window, I could hear her relieved rush of breath.

We were happier when Michael was with us. But for my mother, and therefore for me, this happiness was a fragile thing, like the surface of water, and a small event or certain words of Michael's could provoke waves of distress in her. I realized that my efforts helped very little, though I didn't stop trying to be good and quiet, because it was this behavior that she encouraged and that calmed her.

When Michael was offered a job in New York, he left without us. My mother found out she was pregnant sometime after, and he sent her a check.

My mother told me once that she felt at home in Sausalito and Mill Valley. She and Kathy called everything else "Pepsi-Cola Land," the land of the fifties, of plastic and old-fashioned songs and phony lives on TV. Other towns, even ten miles away, were full of the neighborhoods and shops that reminded them of the home they had left in Oregon, drawn to the music and ideas of California in the sixties. Here they could do anything and live any way they wanted.

Not long ago I came across a photo of my mother from this time. Through it I came to see that my impression of her had been wrong, at least in one sense.

It's an odd picture—she is relaxed, but the setting is dangerous. She's at the Gate 5 marina, sitting in a wicker chair on a narrow gangway that runs parallel to what looks like a dock. She wears cropped gray pants and a man's plaid shirt. Her hair is shoulder-length, and though her face is tipped down, her beauty is unmistakable.

The gangway is connected to the dock by a few wooden planks, nailed down haphazardly. It's missing a few planks itself, and at the edges it is darkened with water, since the gangway is half sunk into the bay. The water is only inches from her bare feet, and one of the chair legs is close to a gaping hole. It looks as if she could drift off at any moment, or sink, swallowed by the bay and pulled out to sea.

But she calmly reads a newspaper in the bright sun, which makes stark shadows beneath her. The picture is startling because it is one of only two pictures I have of her when she is still, not talking or gesturing. In my memory of her, she is in constant motion. My mother's energy was like a thing unto itself, and separate from her; she seemed to use it as a shield, as protection. But here is proof that she rested.

This is her life: amid shambles, she remains unaffected. She is adventurous, lacking in common sense, even selfish. So the image remains—my mother in a precarious, dangerous spot, yet she ignores it. She will do as she pleases.

It's not surprising, then, that my mother taught me to be independent. I was supposed to follow her on the street or inside a store—she purposefully walked away until I learned not to lose sight of her. She didn't like mothers who yelled after their children. When I was three years old, I began to go to the 7-Eleven alone to buy groceries. In the beginning she watched from the window to make sure I looked both ways before crossing the street. With me I would carry some money and a note in my pocket. I couldn't read, but my mother would help me memorize what she'd written on the note:

Wheat bread
Peanut butter
Milk (quart)
Winstons or Marlboros

Sometimes, in the afternoons, I walked to the top of our street, to the park, where my mother would meet me later. Easterby is a short, steep street, and I'd keep to the sidewalk as I'd been told, climbing my way up, stopping to turn around and rest, and to see if she was coming yet. From halfway up the street I was high enough so I could see the bay and the houseboats where I knew Kathy lived.

I loved the tiny park, which I thought of as our own—there was rarely anyone else there. Tucked away off the street, it was quiet and dim, shaded and sheltered by giant trees, the grass tender and thin. Shaped like a key, the park opened up at the far end, where there was a high, curved fence, and beyond that, a creek. There wasn't much—a round patch of sand, a small swing set, and a miniature horse and elephant on giant springs. I liked these animals, which wore brightly painted saddles and excited expressions. They were frozen in a jumping position, as if forever trying to escape. It took a while to get myself situated because I was so small, and because they swayed and bobbed impatiently while I climbed onto them.

I would ride first the horse, then the elephant, then the horse again, gripping the cold handles, and there I would stay, rocking each back and forth and back and forth, faster and faster, the world a kaleidoscope around me, until my mother came.

Gate 5

Each morning on her way to work in San Francisco, my mother walked me to the Gate 5 marina, where houseboats sat like broken ships on the bay. She lowered me in a basket to her sister, my aunt Kathy, on the dock below. Kathy, a pretty, skinny girl of twenty-one, wore suede miniskirts and shawls and believed my daily visits gave her life meaning. She rented a houseboat called *The Love* for a hundred dollars a month, with no running water, and sometimes the lights worked and sometimes they didn't.

Gate 5 was our playground for a couple of years, until I turned four. It was a maze, it was Alice's Wonderland, and we often got lost. This was a place where children had drowned. But Kathy took care of me. I hated wearing shoes, so she watched for nails, rusted pipes and rails, and the missing planks under which the dark bay surged and swayed. Narrow docks ended abruptly; others flooded at high tide, and then we had to climb gates and journey over abandoned ferries or someone else's boat. Some places you couldn't get to unless you were shown the way, but it didn't matter if we got lost because there were always new and old friends and music and pot and everyone loved us.

Some nights Kathy cocktailed at the No Name Bar. That's where she met her boyfriend, Tim, who lived in the steering house of a

1970: Star, Mac, Joelle's mother, Joelle's aunt Kathy, and Joelle

barge. Tim was lean and dark, and he wore a dark blue coat with the collar pulled up like wings, framing his face. He played his drums every night, and one time a new neighbor got mad and shot at Tim's boat with a rifle, but Tim just played an extra-long set that night, then painted a giant FUCK YOU in black on that side of the barge.

At Gate 5, wild dogs roamed the docks, they knew their way around, and one time a Great Dane called Mondo scared some guy, wouldn't let him pass, and the guy jumped right into the bay. My favorite was Dog Hopper, a black Lab who would walk along the railroad tracks to Sausalito and then sit on the corner and wait for a ride back to the houseboats.

The highlight of the day for Kathy and me was watching the helicopters land at the heliport. We'd hear the helicopter first—that high eerie sound, leathery wings beating—and then we'd find someone with a car and drive like mad to the landing pad. The helicopter hovered above us, the wind tearing our hair up above our heads, slamming our eyes so that tears tracked down our dusty skin, stole under our clothes. And above the wild, noisy rush of all this, I could hear Kathy screaming in a frenzy, her arms reaching as if to grab the helicopter out of the sky.

But most of our time was spent uneventfully, listening to music and drawing and sitting around with friends, everyone smoking pot. The tides marked time for us. As the water receded, a black moss of tiny flies would cover the steaming shore, which stank ripe as a barn in summer. Near the docks, raw sewage pooled and reeked. Seagulls would stand atop the pilings, turning slow, patient circles as they searched for food and cleaned their gray wings. High tide was better. Once, at a friend's houseboat, a sunken barge, we came early and hung out until we were ready to eat. As we sat around the narrow wooden table, the tide began to come in. It was a full moon that night, so the water was very high. By the end of dinner, the bay water had covered the floor, reaching almost to the tops of our toes, and we had to lift our feet up onto the couch. We couldn't go home until the tide went out, but no one cared.

Sometimes I stayed overnight with Kathy, and I fell asleep to the marina sounds, the groan of rope, the jingling of the lines in the harbor north of the houseboats, and, on windy nights, the small slap of waves. During a full moon the water was calm and placid, reflecting the boats and their masts that rose like stalks in the night. And always the houseboats whispered and creaked against their moorings, reminding me of vague complaints, as if the boats were always trying to find a more comfortable position. Even the docks shifted slightly on their bed of water. The marina seemed wholly alive to me, a being with as many rhythms and habits as the people who lived there, as the gulls who made their nests within its wooden cracks and cradles.

It was silent only when the tide went out. Then the boats would settle into the muddy bay, rising again hours later, like toys in a slowly filling bathtub.

See us there as we look for someone's houseboat where we'll find friends and music and pot and maybe juice. I take hits off joints like everyone else; my beers come with a straw and my wine in a cup. Kathy dresses me in velvet and hoopskirts and ties my hair in ribbons, and men carry me on their shoulders and tell me stories. Any man, every man, could be my father.

I was loved. I had no bedtime. I fell asleep on laps and couches and on piles of coats, and sometimes a dog or another kid slept beside me. I was never alone.

Miss America

In the June mornings I painted Hawaiian flowers, watercolors of red hibiscus and yellow plumeria, my mother's favorites. The watercolor set was a gift from my grandmother, for my sixth birthday the month before. I liked the rhythm of my days, the early hours spent with brushes, their wet cold tips, the first splash of color on white paper, the shades I discovered when yellow touched red, then seeped into blue. I loved the smell of chalky paint, which got thin and watery and washed away if I wasn't careful.

Each painting was of a single flower, and it would fill the paper, the petals wide open and reaching.

My mother would kneel beside me, smiling at the artwork and also at my ability to entertain myself. This was the way she liked me best: content, engrossed in an activity. When I finished, I'd lay the paintings out to dry in rows on the deck, placing a stone on each corner to keep the paper flat. The deck was then covered with giant flowers. From the kitchen window, I proudly watched this garden.

After lunch I rolled the stiff paintings, and my mother helped me tie each one with a ribbon. I'd say goodbye to her and my new father, Mac, and carry them in a bag to Bridgeway Street. There I sold them for fifty cents apiece, and spent the money on bubble-gum ice cream and red licorice.

. . .

We lived on a hill, and there was no direct way to Bridgeway, but instead an intricate maze of narrow, curving roads that often led to dead ends and short streets that stopped at parks or driveways. Heading downward, I would eventually find Princess Street, which spilled out onto Bridgeway at the bottom, but the opposite was not true: as I worked my way upward from Princess, the streets didn't all lead home, so I had to be careful to follow the right path. One wrong turn could greatly lengthen my walk or leave me utterly lost, and I would have to retrace my way to the bottom and begin again.

Even so, I loved the walks. Every time was different. The streets were quiet, just the sound of birds, and I kicked acorns that scattered like marbles. The pavement was crisscrossed with tar, lightning-bolt strips that made no sense but whose random patterns were pretty and reminded me of macramé designs. Sometimes I squatted down next to one, my knees making a tent of my sundress, and touched the smooth, sunwarmed tar. On some streets, I could see through breaks in fences and, through windows, the bay and San Francisco beyond.

Bridgeway had always been my favorite place. It was never too far of a walk, though we had lived in a few different places in Sausalito. A necklace of a street, Bridgeway swooped for almost a mile along the edge of Sausalito. One side of the street was lined with stores and restaurants and bars, the other by People's Park and a long stretch of boulders, against which the bay heaved and splashed. I sat on a bench by these boulders, where I could watch the birds—the seagulls, and the pigeons with their satiny green throats. Across the bay, San Francisco looked like a saucer piled with toy buildings. The Golden Gate Bridge was just around the corner, though I couldn't see it. Seagulls crawled up the sky and then plunged to the ground, strutting and squawking along the rocks.

On Bridgeway Street, every day was a street fair, a carnival, and I was part of it. Musicians played on street corners and in doorways, their songs surrounding me, then fading as I passed, replaced by others farther on. I moved through music as if swimming in and out of warm ocean currents.

In the park, people sat cross-legged on blankets. Like me, they sold things they'd made, beaded necklaces and medicine bags and carvings. Someone would call me over, give me a handful of beads, a leather ribbon. Another would trade me a drawing for one of my paintings. Most knew my name, were happy to see me. Some got too close, touched my face, kissed my cheek, smelled my hair. I would pull away gently. I was used to the way strangers seemed to love me, though I was always a little surprised at first, and overwhelmed. It was something about my face, my hair, my smallness. I didn't seek it out, not directly, but maybe that was one reason I came to Bridgeway so often that summer, for the affection I found there. I gathered the attention, stored it inside me. I always moved on, though, because I didn't belong with these people, friendly as they were. Despite all the people around me, there was never any doubt that I belonged to my mother. My attachment to her was fierce. Still, I never insisted that she come with me—I didn't whine or plead. The most certain way to her heart was to be self-sufficient, as grown-up as possible.

So in my mind I carried my mother's image with me as surely as I carried my paintings that made her proud, and along with her image, I brought the love and longing I felt for her.

People offered me hits off their joints, but I smiled and walked on. I was like the dogs that traveled solo up and down this street. Seen and not seen. People gave us food, petted us, called to us. Yet we were free and answered to no one.

My mother told me to be good each time I left, but she had faith in me. She trained me to think for myself. She thought it was creative and enterprising that I sold my paintings on Bridgeway. My independence cultivated as a reflection of her own. Mac told me all the time that children should be seen and not heard, and he liked that I never raised my voice. I loved him, and his praise, the way it wrapped itself around me, kept me warm.

One day I notice a man is following me, from one end of the street to the other. There's something wrong with him, I can tell. Suddenly he's beside me. He's too friendly, too close. He takes my hand. I look at people who no longer see me. I'm invisible to every-

*   *The Territory of Men*

one but this man, and I am all that he sees. He wants to look at my paintings, the few I have left. In here, he says, and pulls me up to sit with him in a stairwell, a small, dark opening between buildings. He says it's his step, and now it's mine, too.

He puts the paintings down and sets me on his lap; with one arm he circles me and with the other strokes my hair, which he claims is as beautiful as my flowers, even more. Under my dress, my knees poke out round and white, and I hold them tight in each hand like apples. Beneath, my feet dangle in their dirty gray Keds with no shoelaces. Leaning in this close to my face, he calls me "Miss America." I smell the sour-wine stink of his breath as it rides the back of his words.

People walk by, but no one looks up far enough, not when I cry, not when he kisses me, his mouth warm and wet. My face in his huge, huge hands. I don't know what he wants from me. He touches me, and though it doesn't hurt, I hate it. He touches me like the grown-ups who lie together in the park or on blankets on the grass. I can tell he's drunk, but there's something else, something worse. His words are loud, crowding one another. His shivering hands.

There is a place inside that I pull into when I need to, a safe place where I hope he can't reach me. I pretend I don't feel his mouth or see his face. Instead I listen, I nod when I'm supposed to, because if I'm good and quiet enough he might go away. Then, very softly, I tell him I have to go home. My mother. She's waiting for me, please. But, he says, you won't come back. I can't let you go, Miss America. This goes on for a long time. He makes me swear that I'll come back. I have to promise again and again.

I want my mother, want to scream for her. She would tear and claw this man to pieces.

I'm crying hard now, and my nose runs, and he lets me go. I leave the flowers, and with them my days of painting, my love of Bridgeway, on the concrete step.

I run faster and faster up the steep, curving streets, over the dried tar that looks like spilled black paint. I try not to get lost because we live in a new place, and I'm not sure I can find it just now.

5

Naked

M ary was my mother's best friend, and when I was about six, she invited us for a visit. Mac had to work, so it was just my mother and me. Mary and Bob had moved a few hours north of the city, near the seaside town of Gualala. It took us all day to reach it, a long, windy drive, first up the coast and then inland, along the Russian River, until we reached a forest, through which we rolled and lurched over potholed dirt roads, one after the other, up the mountain, until it felt like we were tunneling rather than driving through the shaded woods. Finally, at the top we arrived at a clearing, and beyond that the ocean lay faraway and calm and still until it met the horizon.

When I think of Mary, I picture her naked, since that is how I first saw her, and mostly how she spent that weekend, though she often wore sandals and a black cowboy hat with a strand of beads and feathers hanging over the side. I'd been around naked grown-ups before, on the houseboats and the nude area at Muir Beach, but at home my mother liked people, including me, to keep their clothes on. I couldn't help staring at Mary, which made her put her hands on her hips and rock back and laugh. I liked the way she laughed, it made me feel comfortable. She had an earth-mother body—tanned and round, with a big bottom and long, folding breasts. Her blond hair was so fine and thin that it seemed to move in one single, shiny sheet, a golden waterfall down her back.

She must have been in her late twenties then, and she had several children around my age, I don't remember how many. They blurred with the other kids who were there. The place was full of people—some kind of gathering, or maybe it was always like that, but what mattered to me was that I didn't know anyone.

After we said hello, I staked out where I would sleep, which was a ritual of mine when we stayed with people. At Mary and Bob's, I could choose from the main house, a trailer; a school bus on blocks; and a wooden tower that reminded me of a lighthouse. The tower was enticing, with its stained-glass windows and tapestries and view of the ocean over the treetops, but the older kids had already claimed it. So, it was a toss-up between the beanbag in the main house, which was good for curling up in, and the yellow school bus, with the orange and yellow wildflowers shooting out from under it.

I decided to figure it out later and stuck my pillowcase, which I'd filled with books, clothes, and my stuffed badger, behind one of the couches. This was where I normally slept at parties so I could be close to my mother as I fell asleep, but also safely out of the way.

The kids had the run of the place—inside and outside, the garden, the greenhouse, the chicken pens, the woods beyond. I made friends with Mary's son Travis, who was my age. He had blond hair like me and a pensive way about him that I wanted to be close to. We hung out in the garden, helping to dig up potatoes and carrots and picking snails off the lettuce. This was another thing I tried to do right away at gatherings—befriend someone in case I got lonely or needed a partner for a game. I preferred children, but a grown-up would do.

Travis and I scratched and rolled around with the other kids and the dogs and cats and goats and chickens. I especially liked petting the goats, who spent their time chewing things. We never went hungry—someone was always giving us snacks: hunks of cheese and homemade bread, apples, handfuls of nuts. At one point Mary made a batch of pot brownies for the grown-ups, which we raided, of course, but because the marijuana gave them a bitter taste, I fed most of mine to a dog, so I didn't get too stoned. Instead, I almost made myself sick over balls of peanut butter and raisins and honey, a gooey mess that got all over my hands and that I'd rub off on my pants or, if I wasn't wearing any at the time, on my hips.

It was fun to be naked, to feel the earth and sun on my skin. The grown-ups mostly wore clothes; but we saw them naked when they hosed off, or at night when they went in the hot tub. You could tell who had come from the city, because their butts and boobs would be sunburned by Sunday, reminding me of swinging pink moons and balloons.

During the day the kids accumulated layers of grime and dust, and if you licked a finger and drew your name on someone's bare back, it'd be as neatly outlined as pen on paper. It wasn't important to be clean; it was important to be natural. And what could be more natural than dirt and mud and sweat? The smells! I swatted away passionate dogs that rooted around in this paradise of sticky bodies. More than once I felt the warm, slick swipe of a dog's tongue on my butt.

Later I washed with the other kids in the hot tub, big enough for five or six of us to play in. It overlooked the ocean through a clearing in the trees. During the day the water was warm as a bath, and we used it as a swimming pool, diving for rocks. Of course it wasn't very safe, being so deep, with its steep slippery walls. It smelled odd, too, musky, flavored by bodies and the eucalyptus leaves that floated on top like feathers. I'm sure Mary didn't use chlorine, but a natural-based soap, maybe the kind she kept in a jug next to the hose. And I know I wasn't the only one who peed in there, because the boys would brag about it. We had great fun anyway, hooting and splashing.

At sunset, everyone would stand around to watch the sky change, and though there was laughter and a good mood overall, I began to feel uneasy, the way I always did at nighttime parties. When the sun went down, we went inside and Mary and Bob sang and played guitar, and that was how the grown-ups filled the evening, with music and drink and pot. Bottles clinked in the kitchen—everyone had a glass of wine or beer, and someone passed around some brandy. I liked the apricot kind, but it made my belly burn.

Late at night, it was the grown-ups' time for the hot tub. They stripped down in the living room, the clothes peeled off and left in heaps at their feet. Carrying glasses of wine and candles, they wandered over to the hot tub, their bodies luminous in the candles' glow. The homestead was unrecognizable at night; it seemed to me that black curtains had been draped over the world around us. The children stayed together, an unspoken agreement; we sat on blankets at the edge of the candlelight, in a ribbon of darkness, and just beyond I thought I could hear the forest inching closer. Above us, stars pulsed, white and tiny heartbeats.

We could have done anything, but we wanted to be near our parents. Besides, how could we ignore all those naked people with their strange patterns of hair, dark and swirly-wet? The very size of these bodies left me speechless. And the men, how different they were from Travis, with his tiny, bouncy penis like a rubbery button! It was alarming, too, to see my mother exposed, her pale body and its awkward climb in and out of the water. She seemed both powerful and yet so unsafe in her nakedness, open to danger. What kind of danger? I couldn't say, but I was nervous all the same.

They were high from wine and pot, laughing loudly, having the nighttime good time. The men made me uncomfortable, especially when they called me to them, to their laps, but I never went. I could just see my mother through the steam, submerged in the tub below her shoulders, hair wet and close around her head. Someone passed her a joint, and she breathed a column of smoke straight up to the stars. Sometimes I imagined she and the others weren't real at all, just ghostly shapes that would dissolve when I wasn't looking.

When the water got too hot, the grown-ups would sprawl and crouch on the ground nearby. Steam billowed off their bodies in fierce waves in the night air, and it became hard to tell one from another. Now and then a couple would leave for the house, leaning on each other as they tripped and tiptoed over the naked ground, and we could hear their voices fade, their murmurings.

Eventually all the grown-ups went indoors, where most of them put on some clothing. We would follow and sit out of the way, near the warmth by the woodstove, and the younger kids would fall asleep. The house smelled of meat and bread and marijuana. Someone would bring out the guitars again, and then a man would carefully set up some cocaine on a table, laying out spoon and razor and mirror: the clicking as he chopped the powder, shaped it into a row of white snakes. It always made me think of a game, like Monopoly, but I knew what came next. I decided then, on the first night, that I might sleep in the school bus after all. I didn't like the way my mother's pupils grew so big that they turned her soft blue eyes to black. It was a bottomless black, and if I looked too long, I might disappear, too.

1972: Mac, Joelle's mother, and Joelle

6

Howard Johnson's

Mac was my third father, and with him life got more normal, at least in comparison to the lives of the other kids at school and of those I saw on TV. We moved several times in Sausalito, but he and my mother both had good jobs in the TV business, which meant we could begin to afford nice groceries and clothes and, in the last year, a three-bedroom house, one with a huge willow tree that shaded our yard in a way that to me seemed protective.

Mac was with us for four years, until I turned seven. I called him Dad, but it was not only for his steady presence that I loved him. Although he agreed with my mother that I should have freedom—to sell paintings on Bridgeway if I wanted, or to play alone at home— he also treated me like the child I was, with a loving respect, never expecting too much, and if for example I cried over some disappointment, then that was all right, as long as I didn't overdo it. This was new to me. In my experience, people had taken me for a small adult, much more capable than I was, and I felt the confusing pressure of that assumption like a constant wind.

Mac used to play with me like another child; we'd chase each other around the house, or he'd swoop me up in his arms and give me an airplane ride while I shouted with joy. On the weekends he took me for rides on his motorcycle, and I'd sit in the cradle of his legs as he drove up and down the Sausalito hills and over the Golden Gate Bridge. He taught me to lean with him into the curves, even though my instinct was to resist, to lean the other way. In this and in other ways I learned to trust him. If he saw my scared face in the doorway while he was arguing with my mother, he'd try to reassure me with a wink and a smile. It was as if high spirits always simmered below the surface of any mood.

I loved him, and I loved the idea of him, a father who was kind and fun, who never seemed to tire of me. At school I would picture him at home, bent over his notepad, or coming up the driveway on his motorcycle, just the image of him enough to make any moment more pleasant and secure.

Until we moved to the house with the willow tree, my mother and Mac got along fine. We often went on day trips or out to dinner at Strawberry Joe's or El Rebozo. I'd sit quietly as they talked, content to simply watch and be with them. They seemed to me to be the most beautiful parents—my mother with her dark elegance, Mac with his brown curls and easy grin. The waitress was always pleased to see us, and I believed this was because we were a normal, beautiful family. I knew I didn't look like him, but no one could mistake his fatherly ways—how he cut my food for me or made sure I got another soda if I wanted one.

We also had a dog, a Belgian shepherd named Star, who was in love with my mother. He followed her around with a sad desperation, his tail a sagging flag sweeping back and forth behind him. Star seemed to complete my mother and Mac and me, curled up near us at night when we played Monopoly, or chasing the sticks we threw for him in the river near Muir Beach. Star didn't share my confidence in his role, though, for he was always nervous, as if he knew our circumstances were fragile, and temporary.

I met Josette and Analisa in the fall of the last year with Mac, and it seemed to me they appeared as angels, though I'd seen them before at school and knew they were also second-graders. I was a new student, and instead of going straight home after school, I would play on the playground by myself. It was mostly empty, but I was used to being alone. One of my favorite tricks was to leap from a wooden bench to grab the even bars, and then I would swing like a gymnast. It was quite a jump to the bars, and exhilarating. But one time my hands, dry and warm, slipped off the smooth metal. My feet sailed out through the air in front of me and I landed flat on my back, the force of the fall emptying my lungs in a terrifying *whoosh*. For a very long time I simply lay there, legs and arms outstretched, stunned and paralyzed—unable to breathe.

When I opened my eyes, I saw Josette's and Analisa's faces looking down at me, open and wide as daisies, and above them, swirling white clouds. They helped me to sit up, and smoothed back my hair, and stayed beside me on the bark-covered ground until I was all right again. For that year, until my mother and I moved to San Rafael, I spent every moment I could with these two new friends.

After school we walked home together, usually to Analisa's, where her mother, who was a housewife, made cookies and frosted cupcakes for us. Analisa's mother would call us her "pretty girls," and I liked that we could be described in such a way. Analisa, tall and blond like me, had freckles dusted on her nose and shoulders, and she was nice but kind of pouty. Josette was short and strong and brunette, with big brown eyes. She was much tougher than either Analisa or me, and in our races, whether on bike or on foot, she always won. This didn't bother us because she never gloated, and because we each had our qualities: I could draw and tell stories, and Analisa owned the best games and had the most comfortable room in which to play them.

We slept over at one another's houses whenever we could, though we usually had to manipulate our mothers, which we enjoyed, because when we finally got permission, the feeling of victory gave the evening more weight and pleasure, as if the consent had not been granted to us but surrendered.

We had no interest in boys, except as nuisances to avoid. Our time was filled with games of jacks and marbles and Pick Up sticks, tree climbing and playing dress-up. We took long, meandering bike rides through lots full of tangled blackberry bushes and crisscrossed with tracks of deer and raccoons. We built forts of cardboard and blankets, propped up with old boards and branches. There we sat, surrounded by the smell of honeysuckle vines, the breeze carrying the tangy scent of the bay and the cries of the gulls, the foghorns beyond. And we did this under the maternal watch of Mount Tamalpais, the mountain that rose above Sausalito and all of Marin County, its outline that of a pregnant woman lying on her back. Josette and Analisa were the missing pieces of what for me had become a kind of heaven: a family, a house, and two best friends.

But this heaven began to slip away, though I pretended otherwise. That winter my mother and Mac began to fight. She was six months pregnant with Mac's baby by then, and we no longer did family things. I'd watch her in the backyard, talking and crying on the phone, smoking a cigarette and drinking a glass of wine, slumped in her terry-cloth robe. She always lost the sash, so she'd be held together by a macramé belt or a scarf, her bare feet lost-looking in the grass. I kept my distance because I knew there was nothing I could do.

In the afternoons I played with Josette and Analisa, but when I went home at night, if there was fighting I would escape to my room. When it got so bad I thought the walls might fall, my mother would throw open my door and pull me down the hall and out into the car. Mac would stand in the doorway, calmly watching us go, silhouetted by the light behind him. It became a common scene on our street. Sometimes the neighbors stood at their windows as we rushed over the dark yard, dropping coats and shoes, crying, slamming the car doors. My mother would make the tires screech on the way out, as if she always had to have the last word.

I'd curl up in the backseat, still in my pajamas. Though she'd tell me it was a game, she was always crying as she said it, her face shiny and wild, and besides, I knew by then what was fake and what was real. On the way I'd lie down so that all I could see were the bright streetlights shooting by high above, one after the other, as if the world were spinning so fast the moon passed by each second. At some point she'd say frightening things, like "I want to be locked up in a white room and covered with white sheets and never ever wake up." It was clear to me she meant to be alone in this white place, and I made myself even more good so that she'd consider taking me along.

We ended up at motels on these nights, usually Howard Johnson's, comforted by the familiar orange and brown colors and plastic everything. She'd pay at the office while I stayed in the car, sleepy and a little scared. These were strangely peaceful times, when the world was quiet and dark and seemed to have compressed close around us. I missed Mac, but I couldn't bear their fighting, so the motel was better than home on these nights.

Although I'm sure we never stayed in the same room twice, they all looked and smelled alike, and I began to feel at home in them. They had matching furniture and framed pictures of soothing landscapes, like in my grandmother's house. I liked the flowery bedspreads, stiff and waxy, and the crisp, cheerful pillows, with the faint crackling of plastic when you turned your head. These were the cleanest places I'd ever been in. The bathroom was especially amazing—not even a hair on the floor, and the toilet paper folded to a neat point. In our haste we always forgot the toothpaste or toothbrush, but things like that had never mattered much to us anyway. At least we always had the motel soap, wrapped like a tiny present that fit in my hand.

My mother would take a hot bath and come out with wet hair slicked back, her face rosy and tired but calm. She'd put her arm around me and we'd sit together, maybe watch a little TV from the bed, and it felt almost like a sleepover, though I could feel her sadness between us, so big I could never cross it. That was something only Mac could do. I would imagine him in my mind, wanting the solace and safety he offered, and comfort myself by thinking they would make up, they always had, and that things would get better once again.

She usually fell asleep quickly, the humming air conditioner blocking any sound beyond our room, and it was easy to forget everything outside. I'd listen to her breathe, the rhythm stretching longer and heavier, and I'd try to pace my breathing with hers. Eventually I'd fall asleep, but something would wake me up, some commotion in the room next door or a car in the parking lot, its headlights sweeping the room, reminding me where we were.

Before bed I always made sure to get my lunch money for school the next day, which I set on the dresser, because my mother was forgetful on those mornings. We were always in a hurry, and it was a little embarrassing, in the light of day, to scurry to the car in my pajamas. She'd take me home, where I changed my clothes, and then I'd rush to meet Josette and Analisa on the corner. We walked to school together, like always, and our day would begin anew.

7

Nine Days On, Five Days Off

In my mind, it all happened on the same day, the same afternoon, when I was seven years old: my little brother Dace was born, Mac moved out, and my mother's boyfriend Tom moved in. In truth, my mother had been seeing Tom while she was pregnant with Mac's son, and the changes took place over a few weeks. But my memory has collapsed these events into one, as if they were easier and simpler to carry that way.

Before he left, Mac took me on a motorcycle ride up Highway 101 to Tiburon, a nearby town across the bay. He pulled over and pointed out Sausalito, and the direction of our house, which we couldn't see because it was hidden by the curve of the land. I tried to picture it, but in my imagination it already felt small and sad.

He said we were all leaving that house, but we would not be going to the same place.

He had brought me here to say goodbye. We sat down on a bench, and he held my hands and told me I needed to forget him because he was going far away, and because I had a real father in Hawaii. He said my father was real to me in the way that he, Mac, was real to my new brother, Dace. It had to do with blood. Dace would be visiting him in the future, and I would visit my own father. His voice was calm and low. He didn't look at me much—he'd just glance in my eyes and then quickly away, as if they were too bright to look at. Usually he talked to me face-to-face, and his nervous eyes worried me, though my hands were warm in his. What he had said was so strange—how could I imagine him gone? It was impossible! Here he was beside me. Where would he go? Where would he live? And what I most wanted to ask: how could I make him stay? Questions rose and fell in my mind. I thought if I spoke them out loud, or if I cried, it might upset him and make him want to leave even more. I listened respectfully, hoping he would be impressed by my grown-up manner and change his mind.

It was a faint hope, though, for he made everything sound inevitable and final, as if there was no way to stop it. Still, it didn't make sense. Mac was strong and powerful and good. I believed he could be with me if he wanted, if he loved me enough. I realized that he must want to go. And then he did, that very day, and the pain of his leaving burned a hole in me that would not be filled, though I would try for many years, in many different ways.

At home I kept my distance from Dace, a pink face in blankets, and Tom, whom I disliked intensely: his voice, his smell, his big clumsy movements. My mother became even more important to me. Like our dog, Star, I watched her carefully and always knew where she was. Whenever she looked at me, I felt as if I'd moved into sunlight, but when she turned away, I was suddenly chilled and a little afraid.

One day, walking by the living room, I stopped and watched my mother breast-feeding Dace; I was intrigued and disturbed by their closeness, which I didn't feel much from her anymore. Mac was the one who had held me all the time. She saw me and said that I had done the same thing, breast-feed, as a baby. She asked if I wanted to know what the milk tasted like, offering to put some in a dish for me, and I said yes. I was curious to taste it because it was something special that she did for my brother, and also because I was jealous and lonely for her. She went into the kitchen and came out with a saucer of her milk, which she handed to me, like something you'd give to a cat. I held it in my hands, careful not to spill it. She watched as I sipped the milky gray broth. It tasted warm and strange. I made a face, and then we both laughed at the silliness of it. I was pleased, and in this small way, for a while, I felt connected to her again.

Our new family—my mother, Tom, Dace, and I—moved north to San Rafael, to the first of three houses, and I entered the third grade at Coleman Elementary School. Of all the adjustments I needed to face, Tom was the hardest.

Tom worked on a tugboat, nine days on, five days off, and he returned grizzly and unshaven, clothes stiff from sea spray, smelling of the ocean—a briny, sharp odor I associated with mysteries only vaguely imagined—pirates with eye patches and bloody swords, sea monsters rolling in the dark waves, and men who guzzled whiskey and showered with seawater. He'd call out my name, search the house for me, because from the beginning I tried to avoid him. But of course I'd have to see him eventually. He'd grab me in a bear hug, and where he touched my skin—my hands and wrists, my face—I would taste salt and, beneath, the faint tang of metal.

During the first days he came home, everything seemed a blur. My mother would cook elaborate meals, and after I'd gone to bed, I listened to them talk and drink and play music late into the night. But when it neared time for him to go back to work, they often fought, bitter and violent arguments that frightened me. Sometimes he hit her, once breaking her nose, but my mother was strong and she would hit back. I admired her for this, because Tom was rugged and big, much bigger than Mac. They always reconciled, and then for a while they'd be very loving with each other. He had a nice-looking face, with a thick mustache starting to gray, and long, thick hair he would sweep off his forehead, out of his eyes. I saw him as an enormous man who could lift me with one arm, whose voice could shake the walls.

These years were marked by his coming and going, like an uneven tide that transforms the land, flooding it and then leaving it strewn and empty. It was a strange rhythm to live by, and I never quite got used to it.

. . .

I learned right away that Tom was like the mean boys at school, the bullies, the ones who enjoyed making other kids cry. This threw me, because Tom was a grown man in his thirties—I had no idea how to deal with him. He liked to play with me and Dace, to tease us, as he called it. When my mother was gone, he would set me on his lap and poke me with a stiff finger over and over in the same places: the back of the knee, under the arms, on the stomach. He made me sit still while he did it, or else I would be denied some privilege, like going to a friend's house after school. Sometimes the teasing was just for "fun"; other times it was a punishment that he seemed to enjoy, a chore he looked forward to. He wasn't like most adults, who in my experience didn't like disciplining children. Tom did, the way a person enjoys beating someone else at a game. It meant something to him that I didn't understand, and this scared me.

Even though Dace was only a toddler, Tom would pull his ears, which stuck out a little, just enough to make him howl. He never went far enough to hurt either of us, though as Dace got older, he would yell and thrash; I didn't know how to do that. It felt strange and futile to fight, and it didn't work anyway. A handful of times, for no reason I could ever see, Tom would stop and just hug me, as if he was suddenly sorry or had felt a wave of affection. I hated this as much as the teasing, maybe more. I sensed that if I returned the affection, or even acknowledged it, he might go easier on me, but I couldn't—I felt no love for this new father. I wouldn't give an inch, no matter what it cost. Most of the time I just avoided him. He moved quickly for a large man, but I got better at hiding as the years went on. I knew how to slip into closets without making the hangers clang, deep in the folds of my mother's dresses and coats. I had another hiding place, a sort of compartment in the stairwell, where I made a nest, laid out a blanket, and kept a flashlight and some books, which were my best form of escape.

Mornings, getting ready for school, were the worst. Tom had embraced the seventies health craze, and he took my brother and me on like projects. He planned to make us strong and healthy, as if we weren't already. Each morning he methodically laid out our vitamins, sometimes seven or eight kinds. These were not sweet children's vitamins, but great foul-smelling pellets of kelp and alfalfa and chalky zinc, and they scraped as they went down, leaving my throat raw and swollen. He would put one hand on my jaw to hold me still, and when I gagged, he'd pour juice down my throat. Sometimes he'd scoop brewer's yeast into our orange juice and, impatiently tapping the counter, tell us to hold our noses when we threatened to throw up.

We ate only organic food at home. Spinach pasta, raw cheddar cheese, unfiltered goat's milk. To school, I brought lunches of natural peanut butter and raisins on thick black bread and sometimes a carrot, unpeeled. I'd open my greasy paper bag and watch the other children with their pristine sandwiches of soft white bread and pink bologna, their cellophane-wrapped Ho Hos and Ding Dongs with white angelic cream. I'd take little things from home—key chains or lipstick or pocket change—and try, usually in vain, to trade for parts of my classmates' lunches. My favorite times were the holiday parties at school where I gorged myself on everything from chocolate Kisses to jelly beans. Sometimes I would save enough money to buy a package of Wonder bread; hiding in the school bathroom, I'd roll each slice into a moist marble before popping it into my mouth.

I had one friend, Nicole, and from the first day we saw in each other our outsider status. It seemed to come down to a matter of association: if your parents were strange, you were strange. Normal kids recognize weirdness in parents right away, figure out which kid they'd never want to go home with after school. My classmates were, for the most part, normal, coming from straight, upper-middle-class parents, people who had respectable jobs as doctors and teachers. My mother was in real estate but more into EST, palm reading, and alcohol. Nicole alternated weeks with her longhaired musician father in Sausalito and her artist mother who wore peasant dresses. And so from the start, Nicole and I were weird because our parents were weird.

I suppose San Rafael was far enough away from the drugged-out hippie world of Sausalito to have escaped its lingering effects. The fog that lay over the bay and Mount Tamalpais, the fog that seemed to hover over my early childhood, dissolved by the time it reached San Rafael. Here the sun shone forever, lending a clarity to the rules by which people behaved.

Nicole and I both liked to read and write, and we became furtive note-takers. We'd sit on the edge of the handball court with a serious, important air and take notes on our classmates. Mainly we tried to figure out the popular girls' secrets. *April 10, 2nd recess: Holly uses Bonne Bell lip gloss, strawberry flavor.* Though we didn't get teased, we must have looked ridiculous, sitting on the sidelines, legs outstretched, looking up imperiously, then bending down again to scratch away in our journals.

After school I'd take my notebook into the neighborhood—having just read *Harriet the Spy*—and I'd crouch behind garbage cans or perch in trees, hoping to chronicle the mysterious goings-on of Coleman Street. But usually what I discovered was so boring I'd end up dozing, after writing *4:45 P.M.: Mr. Adams's dog, Peanut, raids our compost pile.* Even though I was worthless as a spy, I was at that blissful age when just the activity was enough. It didn't matter what I did, as long as it was mine. In fact, I was a bit smug about the spying, and when Tom was away, I took to carrying my notebook around the house with a proud importance.

My sneakiness would increase when Tom was home for his five days. I'd hide from him every chance I got, and as I grew older, I began to steal snacks from him. He had ordered dozens of cases of special energy bars, hefty vanilla- or chocolate-flavored bars coated in a thick carob glaze. He doled them out rarely, according to his rules. He knew I liked them, though I feigned indifference, and he'd eat them in front of me with a lot of lip smacking. They tasted like candy bars that had been on the shelf too long, and you couldn't eat them without some kind of liquid to wash them down, but compared to the rest of our food, they were a real treat. It didn't take me long to find his hiding place, a dusty shelf in the garage, and I'd pilfer them whenever I could, gnawing off the coating and then munching on the insides. I was sure Tom would torture me if he ever found out. But I couldn't help myself. They tasted good, and so did the pleasure I got from outsmarting him.

Then came my downfall, the Girl Scouts cookie sale. After learning that Holly and Nancy had joined Troop 110, Nicole and I
signed up. I wasn't cut out for the Girl Scout life—I was a thief and
a spy, after all—but it was worth a shot. My mother, to her credit,
was all for it, and I got my uniform and books. I was proud of the
uniform, the jumper in soothing green, the prim little blouse, the
beauty-queen sash. Everything fit neatly together: I felt like a
matched set of dishes, not that we had any in our house. But Tom
would tease me without mercy, prancing around the living room,
wearing my sash around his neck like a ridiculous ribbon. I rolled
my eyes because I'd learned that he needed some kind of reaction or
he wouldn't stop. Giving in and crying never worked, either. I had
to show that I noticed, but not too much; the trick was to bore him
without offending him.

Girl Scouts required a lot of energy, all kinds of forms and rituals
and meetings to prepare for. My mom and I were always behind or
late, and I had the feeling that my membership was a shaky one, that
I was always one screwup from being cut. I got only the loser
badges, the ones that didn't take much work, like the Talk badge,
which required easy tasks like doing a "body-language study" and
pretending to meet someone for the first time. The honorable
badges were so demanding, some involving ten steps or more, that
I didn't even begin them. I could never corral my mother long
enough to take me to the courthouse to interview someone, say, for
the You and Your Community badge. But I managed to slip through
until the cookie sale, the biggest ordeal for the Girl Scout. Though
it's shrouded in joyful ceremony, the competition is ruthless.

One day, Holly's mother dropped off fifty colorful boxes of
cookies: peanut butter, mint creme, shortbread. My favorite was
Thin Mints: the thin cookie crisp, the tart cream, all smothered in
smooth chocolate. My mouth watered just looking at them. Who
would notice the absence of one box of Thin Mints? I immediately
stashed one under my bed. I had three weeks to sell the rest of
them. I was shy and a terrible salesperson, and it all seemed like a
big chore to me until I figured out how to connect it to my spying
mission. I could sell them on my own street and gain access to my

neighbors' houses. I could memorize the layout of the rooms and scrutinize people close up. But most of my neighbors, if they bought anything, simply gave me the money at the door and I had to be content with what I could see from there. It was nothing out of the ordinary—Ms. Gilbert was reading *Roots;* the people across the street had bought a new TV. But I wasn't disappointed. Everyone was nice to me, and I liked looking into their homes, even though these glimpses made me feel strangely alone, reluctant to leave.

By the end of the third week, I still had twelve boxes of cookies left. I had sold twenty-eight boxes and eaten ten, most of them late at night, under the covers, and I would wake to a bed full of cookie crumbs and, later in the day, would lick my wrist or inner arm and taste chocolate mint or peanut butter.

Fortunately, the end of cookie sale culminated during Tom's nine days at work, but I was still terrified he'd find out. I figured my mother would be angry, but in some ways she and I were a lot alike, and I knew she'd bail me out. I begged her not to tell him, and she, by this time wanting to avoid any more trouble with him, agreed. In the end my sales ranked respectably, after my mother forked over about thirty-five dollars for my share of the cookies, but we both decided that we had better things to do with our time, and I left my troop with only a little regret, and the lingering scent of sweet mint.

When Tom was home, I took off to Nicole's house if I could. Her mother worked part-time and was always home, bent over some project or other, when we arrived from school. Like a purring cat, she was a pleasant part of the atmosphere. She'd prepare wonderful snacks for us, all laid out on the table or on a tray in the backyard: graham crackers and peach slices and homemade ginger snaps, and to drink, chocolate milk or grape sodas in frosty glasses, with straws, no less. In the pantry lay stacks of breakfast bars filled with peanut butter and fudge and caramel and topped with nuts. I could always get Nicole to grab a few for me, though she never understood my obsession with treats.

I still dream about her house, her yellow room in the converted attic, the soft scrape of eucalyptus branches on the roof, the prism of afternoon sun dancing through lace curtains, and the plush braided rug pushing up between my toes.

My mother and Tom began to fight more and more—there might be one good day out of Tom's five at home. Usually they fought in their bedroom, where I'd hear alarming thuds and crashes and horrible, frantic arguments. One time he chased her out of the room and down the hall into the living room. He grabbed her and clamped her over his knee, yanked down her pants, and spanked her white bottom with loud, fierce slaps while she screamed and kicked. Star leaped onto Tom, insanely barking and growling. Terrified, I ran out the front door to get our neighbor, and on the way out, I passed my brother, who stood in his pajamas, thumb in his mouth, eyes wide. The neighbor called the police, and within hours, Dace and I were on a plane to Portland to stay with our aunt Barbara for a couple of weeks.

When we came back, the house was full of boxes. We were moving again, this time to Mill Valley, the town next to Sausalito. Tom would live down the street from us in his own house. This was good news—we'd see him less. But I was sad to leave Nicole, who had to stay in San Rafael, which was at least twenty minutes away.

We promised to call and get together as much as we could, but we knew it would be hard, and that it wouldn't work out much of the time, and we were right.

At Mill Valley Middle School, I entered the sixth grade. I was now ten, and my body had started to develop, and even though there wasn't much to see, it still alarmed me. I was also becoming more aware of others' bodies, of the different breast sizes of women and the older girls at school. Things I hadn't noticed before now seemed to surround me. Men looked at me differently, even strangers, and older boys yelled insults. This didn't happen often, or any more to me than it did to other girls, but it was enough to put me on guard.

I'd ride my bike home from school, and sometimes I played at the elementary school playground near our house. It was mostly empty at that time of day, but I liked that. One day I saw a man about fifty yards away. He was simply standing there, motionless, facing me. He must have just emerged from the thick brush and blackberry bushes at the edge of the field that spread over nearly an acre. I knew there were trails and tunnels in those bushes, and it scared me—the idea that he might have crawled through them. He was young, and he wore a green army coat and jeans. There was something patient in his stance, and disturbing, like if he was waiting for me according to some agreement I didn't know about. I tried to ignore him, to just play as if everything were normal, but his presence was so unusual, a strange man alone. The world had been reduced to him, me, and the empty school. Then I glanced over, and to my horror, I saw that he had lowered his pants to below his hips, calmly displaying his dark, naked crotch. I whirled away and ran across the empty school grounds, looking over my shoulder every few seconds, but he was gone. And I knew I could never go back to play there again, at least not alone, because now it belonged to that man.

I never told anyone about this incident, and when Tom's teasing became sexual, I kept that a secret, too. He was very interested in the changes in me. He made fun of my Shaun Cassidy records, and after he saw me dancing in my room one afternoon, he'd throw open my door at random moments to try and catch me at it again. He mimicked me when I looked in the mirror, said I'd better eat healthy if I wanted to keep my figure. I tried to ignore him, but sometimes it was impossible.

The first time he touched me, he had given me a ride home from a friend's house, and we were sitting in the car outside my mother's house. As I gathered my things, Tom reached over with his big hand and pinched what little chest I had. Then he said nastily, "Getting pretty big there." I yanked away, my body filling with a sickening rush of shame and shock. I'd been used to his school-bully routine for years, but this act was incomprehensible to me. He was a grown-up, and even though he and my mother weren't married, he was supposed to be my stepfather. Humiliated and flushed with confusion, I ran to the house.

I didn't tell my mother at first. The secret was too horrible to share. To voice it meant I'd have to tell her that her boyfriend had touched *me* the way he might touch *her*. What would she say? It also meant I'd bring more attention to the changes in my body, which was the last thing I wanted. Over that year, Tom continued to poke and pinch and fondle me—but always on the sly, always so that an onlooker could mistake it for innocent roughhousing.

Then one day he took Dace and me to the school playground. I figured with Dace around that Tom would leave me alone; I'd just play by myself in the opposite corner. It was empty except for a couple of kids on roller skates. I climbed on the parallel bars while Tom and Dace, who was now four years old, played on the jungle gym. The parallel bars were high off the ground, and I was making my way from one end to the other, straddling them with my legs while pulling myself along with my arms. Then I heard Tom's voice and saw that he was coming toward me. I looked around but saw no one. It was late afternoon; the school buildings were abandoned. I felt incredibly trapped, exposed. I didn't have time to get to the other side, and it was too high to jump down, even if I could maneuver myself out of my awkward position. Then Tom was under me, his huge face in an ugly grin, and he began rubbing his hand back and forth over my jeans, between my legs. I began to cry with fear and disgust—I couldn't fight him off or I would fall. I just yelled at him to get away, get away, kicking as much as I could, and the words echoed over the concrete of the school grounds and disappeared.

That night I told my mother. I was afraid, but I had no choice other than to trust that she would believe me. She listened carefully, staring at me as if she were reading my face. Her reaction surprised me: she was very calm. I expected sobs and screaming, her wild gestures. Then she told me to get in the car. She walked stiffly, like she was having trouble walking, and when she got in, I realized she was tense with rage.

She drove the block and a half to Tom's house. She was silent and grim, but I felt no anger toward me. At Tom's, she stopped the car.

"Stay here."

I watched her walk to the door, step over the dirty welcome mat, and then vanish inside. I felt calm myself, though I knew I could expect any sort of craziness—any moment she or the both of them could fly out the door. Maybe he was beating her up in there and I would see a window shatter, watch as glass blew out over the yard. But then she came out, and I saw Tom's shadow inside, and the door shut behind her. In the car, she told me that I wouldn't have to worry about him anymore.

I realized that she had chosen me over him, and I felt a love for her so big I wasn't sure I could hold it inside. She reached over and held my hand, squeezing it tightly, enough so that it hurt, but I didn't mind one bit. In a matter of days, my mother, Dace, and I moved to the Oregon coast, where we began a new life, where things were good for a while, where the only tides that marked my life were the ocean's.

Fifteen years later, I ran into Tom at a mall in Larkspur, California, and didn't recognize him at first. His hair was pure white, and there was a frailty about him that made me feel strangely sad for him, but I was only polite, and as soon as I could, I said goodbye. There were many things I could have said, and sometimes I think about them. I didn't tell him that in spite of him, I have a healthy diet, and I take vitamins every morning. They are small and smoothly coated, and when I swallow, it doesn't hurt at all.

8

The Forest King

In 1976, my father drove a cab in San Francisco, and when business was slow, he'd take my little brother Ken and me and drive us around the city. That year, I was ten and Ken was six, and we would sit in back like we were real taxi passengers, and people would look at us, making us feel mysterious and important.

With a cigarette in his left hand, our father pointed out the city's sights: Coit Tower and the Mission District, Fisherman's Wharf and the gay men on Castro and Polk streets. He said he found stories for his book all over this city, that that was why he'd moved here, and why he drove a cab. Ken and I stared at it all, full of questions for our father, who knew everything. He loved San Francisco, was proud of it. He'd say to me, "You were born in this city!"

Subbing for a chauffeur one night, he picked us up in a limousine. He toured us through Pacific Heights and then looped Union Square. My brother and I sprawled in back on the wide leather seats and drank 7UP from champagne glasses. I'd never been close to anything so luxurious. When we stood up and stuck our heads through the sunroof, the wind pulling tears from our eyes, I remember the shock of how the world looked different to me from the inside. Even the stars were closer.

In December he'd take us through the marina where the rich

1976: Joelle's father and her brother Ken

people lived, to see all the Christmas trees and decorations in the big picture windows. The houses were the colors of seashells—cream and white, pale pink and gray. It was grand, there was no other word for it. Some were so beautiful we'd make him stop the car, and my brother and I would press our faces against the window of the cab, our breath making cold circles of fog on the glass.

Although I wished I could live in one of those houses, I never made any connection between my father and the fact that such a way of life was out of our reach. I thought he drove a cab because he wanted to. In fact, I began to think of all of the bay, from Mill Valley to the Golden Gate Bridge to the city itself, as my father's land.

As fun as those cab rides were, I was always glad to go back to his house in Mill Valley, high in the redwood trees, where I stayed with him and Ken every other weekend. The house sat on the steep hill like a shelf, always shaded, enveloped in mist, and spots of sunlight played over the deck like flashlights. This was where my father sat, writing in his notepads, his red flannel shirt like a flag signaling to us at the bottom of the narrow, wooden stairs that led all the way up from the street. He'd left Hawaii to come here, to write his novel. But even more, this is where he was trying not to drink. It was the only time he would be sober in my life, this year and a half, but all I knew was that there was a peacefulness around him, and that when I was near him, I felt it, too.

I'd wake to find him lying on his back on the couch, content as an otter with one of his library books cracked open on his chest. He must have read two or three a week, big hardbacks with plastic covers, and that crackly sound of plastic that I forever associate with him—that and the *whoosh-scratch* of the matches he lit for his Kool cigarettes. As soon as he saw me, he'd greet me with a grin and a hearty "Joler!" as if he hadn't seen me in weeks, and then he'd ask me what I wanted for breakfast. After my brother got up, he'd tell us to go play in the park so he could write, but not before we begged him to tie pillowcases around our necks, so that we had capes, and the superpowers that came with them. In some ways, even though he was almost five years younger, my brother became my best friend after Nicole and I lost touch.

Down the long steps we ran, taking them two at a time, and at the bottom we dashed across Manning Street, skidded and slid down to the creek, and leaped from stone to stone to the other side. We were entranced by the giant redwood trees deeper in the park, whole groves of them. They formed rough circles, natural cathedrals reaching to the sky, their branches wings. Underneath it was hushed. Not even the rain could reach us. Some of the trees were hollowed out and big enough for both of us to hide in, furred over with a green moss that softened any edges. Each could be a cave or a spaceship, a hiding place for runaways. Leaves and feathery redwood bark knitted a quilt over the spongy, moist earth. We hid our shoes and stalked each other like Indians in our bare feet. Then we ran, capes billowing behind us, brandishing sticks, fencing each other and small trees, jumping over benches and rocks. Ken was feisty and fast, but I was just as quick as we traveled all over our father's kingdom.

We always played until dark, until we could hardly see, and came home smeared with dirt, clothes moss-stained, hair damp and wild. Our father would get us cleaned up as he listened to our stories. All day he'd heard us shouting and laughing, our voices drifting up to him. He loved to see us coming—I could see it in his face, hear it in his voice as he called out our names. In some ways our father was the same age we were—childlike, on the edge of something. He was only thirty-six, he still had a chance to achieve his dream. I think he knew he had to be sober to do it. How much did he believe in himself? I wonder if he knew what was at stake, that he would also lose Ken, who would end up going back to his mom for a while. What if I could go back: what could I have said to convince him to keep trying, keep writing, not drink again? Even if I had known the words, would he have listened?

Then one day my father came to pick me up, and there wedged between his legs was a glass full of ice and something else. My mother saw it and told me to go back in her office. My father got out and leaned against the car. I knew they were talking about what was in that glass. Watching them from the window, I could tell all of this: she was nervous and he was trying to calm her, to tell her it was really all right, but she didn't quite believe him. She shook her head and wouldn't look at him. The next time he came for me, he had another drink. No matter what, I was always glad to see him.

I felt the coldness between my mother and father over that summer, as he continued to drink. Whenever my mother came to get me on Sundays, she climbed the stairs and looked around the house, spotted the cans of beer, the fifth of gin on the counter. She didn't say anything to him, but on the way home she'd grill me: What did you do? Did he fall asleep on the couch? Did he eat dinner? Did you?

I didn't know how to tell her not to worry. I couldn't say that she was the one who scared me when she drank too much, not him. When my father drank, he just slowed down like an old toy and eventually wore a silly expression on his face, like some of the handicapped kids at school. Then he'd fall asleep. It bothered me, of course—in fact, I hated it. But at least I felt relatively safe. In the morning he'd always be normal again, cheerful, glad to see me. I never saw him hurt anyone or anything; he never raised his voice or threw things. He was the kind of man who scooped bees out of the house with cups instead of smashing them. I figured if my mother wanted to worry about a man, she should think about Tom, who was as mean as my father was nice.

All of a sudden the drinking was just a part of my father again, the way it was a part of my mother. I remember one Chinese man, a man my father had gone to high school with in Hawaii. He used to bring icy six-packs of beer, and he'd pull one off and toss it to my father and tell him to drink up, what the hell was this sober bullshit anyway? People started coming to visit at night, and most of them were okay. They'd bring food and wine and talk about writing or sports, and they'd always ask about my dad's book, which he didn't seem to look at much anymore. The notebooks, stacked high as my knee, stayed in the corner of the living room.

My father and his friends would hang out on the deck, laughing and drinking, while my brother and I made up and practiced skits inside. I lost myself in these plays and dances, which we performed for our father and his friends. Our father loved this—he'd applaud and laugh until tears came to his eyes. Ken was a ham, flamboyant and funny, and I was clinging to my remaining unself-consciousness. I think these months were the last time I was truly a child. Sometimes our father would put on a record, one of his favorite songs like "I Can See Clearly Now," which he loved for its springy beat, and he'd dance in a happy, goofy way, sliding in his socks, bending his arms close to his sides and puffing them out like wings while Ken and I giggled hysterically on the couch. With my mother and Tom, I rarely let go, but with my father and Ken, I almost always had fun and felt at ease.

Because he drove a cab, my father always had cash in his pockets, and he took Ken and me roller skating, to soccer games, to the Exploratorium in the city. And he liked to take us to matinees, though sometimes Ken's mother or mine would get pissed off because they were too violent or mature for us. But our father ignored them. He wanted to have fun as much as we did. And if he was quiet and distracted at times, I didn't see it. My brother, even though he was only six, seemed to understand our father better than I did. He knew to put blankets over our father when he passed out on the couch, to take away the glasses and empty the ashtrays. Sometimes I'd hear Ken softly singing the Beatles song "Blackbird" to help our father sleep. From my room I would hear Ken's faint, high voice: "Blackbird singing in the dead of night / take these broken wings and learn to fly . . ."

I didn't know how to help my father. Instead I shared the stories I'd started writing, because I knew he loved to write, too, and that made me feel close to him. He encouraged me and gave me advice—he told me to stay away from adverbs: "Look," he'd say, and he'd take a solemn drag on his cigarette, as I waited, watching him. "There's no need to say 'He said sadly.' Don't you see? It's clear he's sad. You don't have to say it."

If this were a story, I'd tell you about the time when all three of us recognized the love we felt. But the truth is there was no revelation, no moment I could point to, no heroic rescue or tearful embrace. There was just the hope that filled that house and the park below, and for as long as it lasted, it was the only thing that mattered to me.

In the mornings Ken and I were eager to go to the park again. We fought villains and saved each other. I was the fairy princess, my brother the elf at my side—and our father, he was the forest king we adored.

9

First Kiss

I was first kissed not by a boy but by Nicole, my San Rafael friend. Whenever I stayed over at her house, we slept in her bunk bed, she in the top bunk, me in the bottom. Eventually, after her parents had gone to sleep and the only light came from the streetlight filtering through the curtain, I'd climb up and join her. We'd whisper and stifle laughter. Finally, one of us would say, "You be the boy," and then, taking turns, we'd practice-kiss.

I remember her body beneath me, on top of me, flat and firm as a boy's, the soft bunching of flannel nightgowns between us, the faint saltiness of her upper lip. That was all we did, kiss with lips tight—we didn't know about tongues. We kissed with a serious concentration, as if preparing for a test. Later, I'd climb back to my bunk, where I could stretch out and sleep comfortably. We never talked about it the next day. It was as if we'd forgotten, in the light of day, about our intense experiments, our dry, heated kisses.

In the summer, after I moved to Mill Valley, Nicole and I saw each other less and less, and then not at all.

Blaine was the first boy who kissed me. He was also in the sixth grade at Mill Valley Middle School, a giant institution compared to Coleman Elementary. It was divided into four sections, each with its own classrooms and teachers: Wood, Wind, Sea, and Fire. Blaine was in Fire and I was in Wood. I didn't know him, but I'd seen him play kickball at lunch with some older boys. He got into fights every so often, and then he'd go off by himself for a while, stroll along the fence or sit on the edge of the field. Because I was a loner sometimes, too, I found this behavior mysterious and attractive. I liked to watch him run—his legs a blur, fast as wings, like he could fly if he really wanted.

Around Halloween, he began to notice me. And one day at recess, like a prince, he sent two of his friends to tell me that he wanted to kiss me, and where, and at what time. The kiss would take place behind the bleachers at Mount Tamalpais High School, where Blaine and I would meet at five-thirty the next afternoon.

I talked it over with my new friends, Lisa and May, and then I sent back a message that I agreed. On my way home from school, I told myself over and over: *He wants to kiss me. He picked me over everyone.*

That night I felt sick to my stomach. Boys were not friends or playmates to me; most of the time they were mean. But I never considered saying no to Blaine. It was already decided, already set in motion. And I knew boys and girls were supposed to be together, and that I would be happier, like my mother, with a boyfriend. I believed I was incomplete, that I was missing something, and I knew instinctively that Blaine could show me what that was.

My friend Lisa came with me. When we got to the football field, Blaine and his friends were already there, sitting on the top row of bleachers where they could see everything, smoking cigarettes and talking. They had a small boom box that was playing a Foreigner song, "Hot Blooded." They pretended not to notice us until we were at the bottom step, and then they ignored us some more. Finally Blaine stood up and looked down at us, scanning the length of me, my Chemin de Fer pants and pink T-shirt that I thought he'd like. He took one last drag of his cigarette, then stubbed it under his shoe. Though he took the steps two at a time, he looked bored. At the bottom step, he cocked his head, indicating for me to follow.

We went around behind the bleachers and walked around underneath, saying nothing, studying graffiti and looking at things on the ground. Candy wrappers and cigarette butts. Dried dog shit. It was dim under the bleachers and smelled old and dank, like a garage. The awkward silence was agony for me. I waited for Blaine to do something, but he seemed to have forgotten me. Through the slats in the bleachers I could see his friends slowly walking around the far side of the track, the music fading with them. Lisa was nowhere to be seen. On the field the sprinklers started up, a *shoo!-shoo!* sound like an urgent whispering audience.

Through the fence behind us I could see the clock tower of the high school. It read 5:35. When I turned back, Blaine was looking at me. I'd never talked to him before.

I said, "What if someone sees us?"

"Like who?"

His voice was surprisingly low, and I realized I'd heard him only when he was shouting on the playground. He pulled his hands out of his pockets, put them on his hips.

"Come on," he said, and reached out one hand to me, like someone who wanted to dance.

I stepped back. "Wait," I said, and smiled. I discovered with dismay that an embarrassed grin had attached itself to my face and I couldn't get rid of it.

"Wait for what?"

He looked around as if to see what I was waiting for, then kicked some dirt over the dog shit.

"I don't know," I said through my grin. I couldn't look at his face. His T-shirt had a faded picture of Han Solo from *Star Wars* on it; the stenciling had started to crack and peel. From its sleeves his arms emerged slim and strong-looking. They were as smooth as mine.

"What's your problem, anyway?"

He twitched his shoulders—his irritation hung on him and he wanted to shake it off. I thought about saying I was sorry, but I knew that would make it worse.

"Nothing, no problem." I said this to the ground. A beer can lay on its side next to an empty balloon that I somehow knew was actually a rubber, though I'd never seen one. It looked ugly and dam-aged.

"Come on, then . . . *fuck.*"

He reached for me again, and again I stepped back. I seemed to have no control. I wondered where Lisa was, even though I knew she couldn't help. I thought to myself: *You're so stupid!* I was hot with shame.

"I just want to know if—" But I couldn't finish, my smile got in the way.

"What? *What?*"

The words flew out before I could grab them. *"I just want to know if I'm supposed to put my arms around you."*

He looked at me for a while, as if he had to translate what I'd said, then with exasperation pulled me to him. He smelled like my little brother Ken—like sweat and Ritz crackers and also bitter, like the red rubber balls we played with at recess. When we kissed, I tasted cigarettes and felt lips softer and wetter than Nicole's. It lasted a few seconds, barely. I didn't even have time to put my hands on his shoulders.

"There," he said, the way you say it when something's finished. He left and joined his friends, who kept looking back and laughing as they walked off together.

I stayed there by myself awhile. I knew this would be the kind of mistake that would follow me everywhere, so closely that I would not be able to see between myself and the mistake. And sure enough, the next day it spread all over the school, the joke of it, and Blaine ignored me the rest of the year and eventually went steady with a seventh-grader named Carla, who knew how to French-kiss and more.

In June my mother, Dace, and I moved to Oregon. I never saw Blaine again, though I've not forgotten the shame of being left there alone, and how I knew even then that the world of men would never be easy for me, that my connection to it would always be touched with a trace of disappointment, and regret.

10

Bonfires

We ran away from Tom to the Oregon coast, my mother, Dace, and I, where for three years we lived under dimmed light. This was our new home, the small town of Lincoln City, where sunlight burrowed through layers of weather, through clouds, mist, fog, rain. One year Mount St. Helens erupted, adding months of smoke and ash that coated our world like gray paint. Sometimes, though, a thread of sunlight broke through the heavy darkness over the ocean, a small but brave gesture. Like a flash of lightning, and just as wonderful and shocking.

As if on a permanent search for a warmer, lighter place, travelers in their Winnebagos and station wagons streamed endlessly up and down Highway 101, which ran parallel to the coast. Our town had no center; its geometry was defined by those two parallel lines of road and water. Tourists gathered on the shore regardless of the clouds, hair matted with sea spray and wind, pants rolled to reveal pale feet and ankles. Although we complained about them and their traffic, they gave us the illusion that we lived in a desirable place.

The dim light was met by a net of cold mist that hung over the town, obscuring the edges of things. Moisture turned salt into crumbs; rust fed on cars like a rash. I'd arrive at school damp, the cuffs of my jeans wet and trimmed with the sand that found its way everywhere. The weather made us: we were resilient, resigned, and constantly searching for warmth.

In this small town, my California roots gave me instant status with my classmates, most of whom hadn't traveled farther than Portland, two hours inland. My clothes were different—I had jeans with bright gold stitching and French-cut T-shirts—and it was assumed I had superior knowledge about manners of style. I didn't, but for a while I got away with it by starting many of my sentences with "In California . . .": such as "In California everyone wears tight pants," or "In California all my friends had hot tubs."

Tish took a liking to me, or maybe at first she just felt sorry for me. I think she saw that underneath my boasting was fear. Pretty, with long, tawny hair, she was the fastest runner in the seventh grade. While most of us were either still tomboys or had become shamelessly boy-crazy and vain, Tish had mastered the art of combining femininity and athleticism without compromising either. More than anything, Tish was cool because of her older brother, Tony, a senior at the high school.

Tony was good-looking, too. When he stretched, his T-shirt lifted, revealing glimpses of a ropy, muscled torso, as if his body were braided beneath. He did all the appropriate guy things, like work on cars and play baseball. He was a stoner, but all the cool guys were. He wasn't home much, but when he was, he stalked the house and made brief, cryptic phone calls, organizing some mysterious mission that Tish and I assumed involved drugs, a meeting with a girl, or some exclusive party for older kids. We were never included in these activities; we were twelve. Tony, however, could tell we would come into our own soon enough, so he didn't completely ignore us. But we couldn't compete with the high school girls and the way they filled out their clothes, and we didn't try.

Tish and I watched Tony. With a lift of an eyebrow or a curl of his lip, he determined what was humorous or undignified, worthy or a waste of time. Aware that his sister's status reflected on his own, Tony checked her behavior like the most exacting etiquette coach. I took my cues from Tish, but they were secondhand, and I didn't get as much practice as she did. It was clear to both of us that I was less cool, but it didn't matter. I was happy to be around her at all.

Our afternoons were spent at her house, a sprawling ranch-style home on a nice street, the kind of neighborhood where the trick-or-treating is good. They had a driveway and a family room. Best of all, the house had central heating and was always toasty-warm. Tish's mother stocked the kitchen with excellent snack material, but we usually settled on vanilla ice cream with Nestlé Quik mixed in, which formed a rich, chocolatey paste that we ate with a fork.

We listened to Tony's albums, rock music like Journey, the Scorpions, Van Halen. The bands had brooding male lead singers with gypsy hair and lean bodies. The passions they sang of we could imagine but were still on the edge of, and we searched for clues to these mysteries. This was before music videos, but we saw pictures in Tony's *Guitar Magazine* of the musicians, legs spread wide, hips poking forward. They screamed and moaned their music as if they were suffering, and we yearned to help. We puzzled over their lyrics, which presented intriguing metaphors such as "the wheel in the sky keeps on turning."

We danced wildly, barefoot on the brown shag carpet of Tish's room, bodies given to the music. We talked about the concerts we would go to someday, how we'd sneak backstage and offer ourselves to these rock stars for marriage and motherhood, for nurturing companionship on those long days on the road.

This music affected boys, too, and we wondered at this. Sometimes Tony would come home, face dark with some teenage burden, and shut himself in his room. Moments later we'd smell the faint scent of pot and hear the pounding beat of Judas Priest's "Breaking the Law," coming down the hall, or Van Halen's "Running with the Devil." Humbled, Tish and I never remarked on it, just gave each other knowing looks. It was clear Tony had experienced the same sorrow that his throbbing music only hinted at.

Tish and I were part of a larger group of girls who were among the more popular kids, a fact that, to me, seemed like a continual stroke of luck. We had slumber parties (but never at my apartment) and played on the basketball team. My seventh-grade year sailed along smoothly until the spring, when all our discussion began to center around the cheerleader tryouts scheduled for May. Next year would be our last at Taft Junior High, and everyone wanted to be a Rascal cheerleader, the pinnacle of success. Making the team also meant certain popularity for the year after, when we would enter high school and become Tigers. The current eighth-grade cheerleaders already hung out with high schoolers at the Dairy Queen during lunch. How we envied them! Some of them even dated high school guys. We knew we were almost guaranteed to have boyfriends if we made the team, and having a boyfriend had become every girl's number one goal, after being a cheerleader.

Underneath all the talk was a sense of anxious dread only whispered about. Because there were just seven spots and about twenty-five girls trying out, some of us wouldn't make it, which led to constant fear and speculation. What was more, each candidate had to try out individually in the gym, in front of the entire school, teachers, and parents, and the student body would then select their cheerleaders by vote. This prospect terrified me almost as much as not being a cheerleader. Fortunately, my mother was boycotting the event on the grounds that it was antifeminist, so I didn't have to worry about her.

My most coordinated friend, Kristin, choreographed my cheer for me, "Tonight's the Night," which was the shortest one I could find. The cheer burst with spunk and urgency, and when I did it right, I added a roll of the *R* in Rascals, like an energetic growl (which was hard to do while jumping around). It went like this:

Tonight's the night! The time is now!
The Rrrrascal team will show you how!
So get it together with courage and might—
Come on, Rrrrascals, tonight's the night!

For weeks I practiced in Kristin's garage after school, until I began to encounter versions of the lyrics in my dreams. The routine, complex and rigorous, required me to contort myself with windmill-like arm motions and to leap from a squat to an exultant full-body Y. To end it all, I had to jump into the jackknife position, but I could never quite extend myself the way it was intended, with one leg shot out in front and—simultaneously—the other arced neatly in back. The move looked alternately abrupt or feeble.

I carefully chose the perfect outfit, so that I would at least look all right: a small T-shirt and cutoff jean shorts over caramel-colored nylons. (We all wore the same brand of nylon, L'egg's, which came in a plastic egg-shaped container; the thick, shiny fabric clung to our flesh like glowing shrink-wrap.) We wore Nike sneakers and anklet socks with a fuzzy ball at the back. We knew this was about appearance, though most of us had the thin, frail bodies of the eleven- and twelve-year-olds we were. We wanted to look like Daisy Mae of *The Dukes of Hazzard.* The overall result was absurd but also somehow provocative. Gazing at myself in the mirror, in my shorts and tight T-shirt, I felt sexy for the first time, felt the power of it.

More than two hundred kids and adults filled the bleachers in the gym; I might as well have been in the Astrodome with a full house, floor to ceiling. I stood there, blood pounding in my ears like surf, and announced into the microphone my candidacy for the Rascal cheerleading squad for 1980–81. Then I did my cheer, and to my surprise, I was wonderful. I was spectacular. I knew it from the second I began and felt it until my final ecstatic jackknife jump, and I heard it in the crowd's booming applause. I didn't want to leave the floor—I wanted to do it again, and then do cartwheels and flips and lead the entire student body in a march through town. I was a Superstar and knew I deserved to be on the team. I've felt such radiant and unadulterated self-satisfaction precious few times since then.

I spent the rest of the day, until the results were posted, in a state of nervous exhilaration. Other kids came up to me, strangers and friends, and assured me I was in. I hung out with the other girls who had done well—Tish and Kristin and Mimi—and avoided those I was pretty sure hadn't made it.

The results were posted after lunch. Before I could get there, I heard someone mention my name as one of the winners, and I froze. I felt like I'd been saved—that for once I not only belonged but it was official.

My joy left me no charity, even when I learned that my good friend Sarah had lost. She wasn't a bad athlete, but cheerleading wasn't about athletics. She hadn't made the team because her head and hands were too big, and her chest was as flat as the slabs of wood we used in shop. Taft Junior High didn't want her representing them. She knew this, too, and posted a heart-wrenching note on Tish's locker, like a manifesto, telling her and all of us that she knew she'd be dropped by us as a friend. Though I felt terribly for her, I also believed there was nothing I could do. I didn't want to associate with such defeat. The realignment of friendships was Darwinian, and I went with the tide.

Making the team wasn't just about looks, though; you could make it on the force of your charm. Mimi, for example, was heavyset, with notoriously foul-smelling feet, but she could pull a party together faster than anyone and had no fear of boys, so she created valuable access to them. Tracey was gawky but relatively rich, and her mother threw sumptuous slumber parties. Tracey also had a certain amount of class that no one could identify but everyone could tell was there.

I understood that my selection was about my looks rather than my personality. This just added to my growing suspicion that my outside was better than my inside. This was the reason I tried out for cheerleading rather than student government—I had no faith in my leadership skills, intellect, or charm.

My mother hated the uniform, which she'd seen in the cheerleading catalog—the tight sweater and ridiculously short skirt. She said it was exploitative, which of course it was, but that didn't matter to me. When I first got the uniform, I wore it at home whenever I was alone, even the socks and black shoes. I'd ignore its scratchiness, the uncomfortable thick polyester fabric, the way the sweater wouldn't stretch or breathe. The skirt with its alternating pleats of black and orange didn't even reach midthigh. When I bent over even slightly, my matching orange briefs showed. Still, I loved it—the proof that I was wanted somewhere.

When my mother first saw me in the outfit, she raised her eyebrows and kind of shook her head. What must I have looked like to her? Thin-limbed, awkward, the skirt too short even though I'd yanked it down as far as it would go. But she knew I was committed, and that she had no choice but to tolerate it. My cat didn't like the uniform much, either; he crapped on it one day, an enormous pile right in the middle of the pure white fabric.

We lived two blocks from the ocean on the upper floor of a two-story apartment, in drafty rooms with odd, sloping ceilings and sidewalk-colored linoleum floors, with a pattern that called to mind cracks and fissures. In the center of the living room the floor rose, like a wave starting to swell. Sand gravitated relentlessly to those floors, so you couldn't go barefoot without stopping to shake off your feet every few seconds. Loggers had lived there before us, drinking and sleeping away their days off, and the place had a strange, sour odor that my mother passed off as the ocean. I always felt cramped in the place, and in the warmer months of August and September I'd sit out on the lawn, which was soft and lush because of the rain, until our landlord dumped a load of gravel over it all to save himself work.

The wet cold of the coast permeated buildings and houses, and ours was no exception. Soft, spotty mold covered the edges and corners of the bathroom and kitchen. It grew furiously, despite our random cleanup efforts, and once I found a cluster of gray mushrooms behind the toilet. My clothes always felt damp in the closet, and in the mornings I froze. I'd turn on the electric heater and stand before it, scorching my front while my back stayed chilled, then I'd spin around and heat my back. I laid my jeans on the heater before putting them on, but sometimes I left them too long, and eventually all my pants had faded burn stripes across the thighs.

As she had with every move, my mother hauled out our knick-knacks and put up the pictures we'd had in all our other houses, which by itself made each place oddly familiar. It always gave me the feeling that we'd been picked up in our sleep, our lives rearranged by a giant swizzle stick, and then deposited in a new town, or in another state.

My room was very small, and the ceiling angled sharply halfway across, so that I could stand up only on one side of the room and sit up only partway in bed. Cold sea air seeped in with a small hiss through cracks in the window seal. My mother spent hours sewing matching curtains and a bedspread. This gave my room a uniform look—I'd always wanted one of those pretty rooms for girls—but the colors I chose were dark, deep red and navy blue, which just made the small room cavelike. At least I didn't have to share it with Dace; he had to sleep in a tiny passageway that led to the back door.

I spent most of my time with my friends. My mother was busy with part-time jobs and college. She was finally finishing her bachelor's, for which she had a long commute to Oregon State University several times a week. When we were home, I'd wrap myself in a blanket and read or listen to the radio with my headphones on. My mother would attempt to start a conversation, and I'd nod at her without looking.

Our years in Lincoln City were the only ones where we lived without a man, but that didn't bring us any closer. Dace and my mother and I rarely did anything together. My mother ran through a couple of brief affairs, but neither moved in. These men, Joe and then George, drifted in and out of the apartment, and she would sometimes stay over at their places. Joe was twenty-one, tall and tan, with big brown eyes. I thought he could be in the movies, or a rock star if he'd grow his hair out a little bit. I'd watch him out of the corner of my eye—looking at him straight on was too much for me. After a few months they broke up. He was too young for her, she said, and listening to my mother cry, I cried, too.

She next found George, an older man who was as homely as Joe was handsome, as if in order to purge Joe from her system she had to choose the most unattractive man in the county. He had squinty, ash-colored eyes and a sharp, mousy face. I thought she was nuts, dumping Joe for George, and it made me feel even more distant from her.

After school, I'd often come back and find her passed out, surrounded by broken glass, unearthed houseplants flung across the floor, as though a horrendous riot had taken place. But I knew it was just her, battling her own demons. I'd glance around and leave for a friend's house, or to walk on the beach, as if I hadn't seen anything.

Years later she told me she broke plants because she loved them, and she wanted to hurt herself for her weakness, for her drinking binges. I believed I was the cause of the drinking, and sometimes I was, indirectly. My brother and I often argued in the morning, and occasionally this set her off. She would yank on her clothes, scramble frantically for coat and keys, and bark over her shoulder, "I'm going to get some bread." We knew what this meant: she was going to the corner market for beer. And I'd say, "But we have bread—we don't need bread! We don't need anything at the store!"

She never looked back. If I was lucky, I wouldn't need a ride or money; if I needed something signed for school, I'd do it myself. I knew I had about fifteen minutes to get out of the house before she returned with two quarts of Budweiser that she'd drink on an empty stomach.

Sometimes I did miss the bus, and the school was four miles away. In the car, my mother's wild rage would tumble over me, a live thing let loose. I pressed my face against the window, and she slapped me without aim or warning. I said nothing; there was no room for my voice, for me. I became a rock on the beach as she crashed over me. Something else had provoked her, something bigger than I could ever be—even in my fear I knew that. I never thought to yell back, to hit back. That was the difference between us. Her anger was a stampede trampling her fear and her pain, and because of it she has always been stronger than I. My anger had crawled into a place deep inside me and crouched there a long time ago, where it would burn for years and years. Deep down I knew my silence goaded her, but I was frozen. I covered my ears as her voice careened through the car, overflowing, escaping through the window seals and hissing through vents.

At the school, I scrambled out. She always sat for a moment, exhausted, silent, tears like silver trails on her cheeks. The place would be empty because classes had begun. As she drove away, I waited until my muscles unclenched and I breathed free again, my heart blank.

I would take a long time to go inside, but the damp cold always got the better of me.

. . .

The summer before eighth grade, my mother announced it was time to get rid of my training bra and get a real one. She took me to the Beach Toggery down the street, which advertised itself as a full-service clothing store for women, but the selection was small and most of the clothes old-fashioned and overpriced. Still, it was all we had, until the Oregon Girl opened up a year or so later on the north side of town. My mother was businesslike about the process, consulting with the saleswoman about style and fit. The two of them nodded thoughtfully while staring at my pitiful chest. A year later I tried to steal a shirt from there but got caught.

My mother told my grandparents that we had successfully acquired my first bra, and they congratulated me as if I'd sewn it myself. Over the next couple of years, my mother and other relatives—not to mention the boys at school—seemed to take an interest in the development of my breasts, remarking on their progress as if they were public property.

The next February, for Valentine's Day, she bought me a pink lace bra and panty set, wrapped in white tissue. We sat at the small table in the kitchen and just looked at it. It was beautiful and seemed almost to glow in our dingy kitchen, with the dirty dishes and the curling linoleum floor. I'd never owned anything like it. Was this what you were supposed to wear with men? I was glad for it, since my mother seemed to think I was a woman. I wanted her to tell me how to use it, when to wear it. It seemed to me a uniform in the same way one might wear a heavy sweater and pants to the beach. But I didn't know what to say. This was my mother's territory, the territory of men. Was there room for me there? Was this her way of inviting me in? Later, I tried it on, but it was too big; the cups gaped and the lace scratched my skin.

LINCOLN CITY IS FOR LOVERS. I had a blue sweatshirt with that proclamation on the front, centered inside a giant heart, and my friends and I spent a lot of time trying to prove it true. My cheerleader status hadn't helped get me a boyfriend, but I never gave up. On Fridays, we went to the movies to find love. The theater, the

Bijou, smelled of popcorn, disinfectant, and wet carpet. Many of the chairs were broken, the velvet threadbare, and broken springs poked mercilessly. But for us, the low light transformed the theater into a place of possibility, where the action in the audience was always more interesting than the movie.

The most important time of the night was the entrance, because that was when you chose your seat, which hopefully would be next to a cute, or at least a popular, guy. If you didn't get a good seat, your evening was ruined—you were stuck on the fringe, your very position evidence that you were outside of things. And a lot could happen in two hours: couples broke up, made up; others started up. Getting a good seat required a vigilant strategy, and it had to be well timed. The window of opportunity ranged from about thirty seconds to a minute. You had to pace yourself while walking down the aisle: walk too fast, for example, and the boy you were tracking might change his mind and sit down earlier than expected; too slow, and another girl could slip in between you. At the same time you had to smoothly fend off the boys you didn't want to sit by, who were trying to sit by you.

My goal, never achieved, was to sit by Chris, who was also in the eighth grade. He was the boyfriend I wanted. Fresh-faced, blond, and smart, he excelled in sports and played a cool instrument in band—the saxophone. He had a normal family straight out of *Happy Days.* Teachers excused him from class to go on field trips for student leaders. I was attracted to the effortlessness with which he passed through life.

But Chris wasn't interested in me—he fell for my good friend Kristin. At home I sat mournfully behind the couch with my headphones on, certain that whoever wrote those sad love songs had secret knowledge of my heart. I thought of his soft muscled chest, the way it had grazed mine in PE, during square dance. For almost a minute we had held each other while the teacher droned on with her instructions, Chris's breath a faint wash over my face, smelling faintly of cake from lunch. I could see him from the corner of my eye, the blond hair a cloud above his blue eyes. Our hands were slick where they met, and I could feel the boyheat of him bundled up inside that smooth white skin. What exquisite agony, standing close, arms locked in the circle of the waltz pose!

We waited for the teacher to drop the arm of the record player, and then the chirpy, scratchy music would begin again and take Chris away with it to another girl's arms. Years later I would be in a political science class with him at the University of Oregon, and he was just as dismissive of me. But by then I didn't care, not very much.

The beach was our other source of romance. My friends and I gathered there when nothing else was going on, which was most of the time. We had no mall, no community center. And at the beach, magic could happen: a baby seal cradled in a tide pool, giant bonfires rising like fireworks on moonless nights, the dunes. We loved to jump twenty, thirty feet down the cliff sides, sinking in soft, dusty sand to our hips. We ignored the weather and just put on another coat. I think I spent half the year with my hood up over my head.

We were forever on the hunt for tourist boys, boys who'd come with their families from Eugene, Salem, Tigard. We'd stroll up and down the highway, or hang out at the Wayside parking lot, perched on the railing over the beach. This was a central location, with a lot of foot traffic, but actually hooking up with the boys was another matter. And if we did connect, it wasn't easy to make everyone happy. No one had money or was old enough to drive, and it was always cold, especially at night. Without fail, there were more of them, or more of us. Someone would be left alone to stroll the beach, pretending to be very interested in the broken shells and driftwood, while couples huddled together among the logs and rocks, out of the wind.

Now and then, on the days my mother was gone, I'd go into her room and shut the door. This was the closest I could get without having to actually face her. It wasn't easy to walk in her room; it overflowed with clothes and shoes, belts and books and newspapers. The dresser drawers pulled out like open arms. Empty cups strewn around the room, on the windowsill, the bedside table. She never made her bed, but sometimes she'd throw the comforter over the lumpy mess of sheets and blankets. Her jewelry box tangled with necklaces spilling over the sides. It was a falling-apart place, but full of life, too. A stranger would think it the scene of a crime, or of a wild act of passion.

I never thought to clean it for her, because I liked it the way it was; changing her room would be like changing her, and I couldn't imagine that. To me, it was a mysterious place where I felt comforted and also alone. Nothing arranged or taken care of, as if none of it mattered to her and she could leave it anytime.

Often I fell asleep and woke to the smell of her, of wool, of ocean and cedar, and I'd lie there awhile, wrapped in the well of her blankets.

I didn't find a boyfriend until I turned fourteen and started high school. Greg, a good-looking senior, wore his sandy hair parted down the middle and feathered back on the sides, creating wings that fluttered in time with his bouncy stride, a combination of ebullience and rock-and-roll style. He walked into a room like he was walking onstage and now that he was here, the show could begin. Going with him gave me immediate status, even though I was only a freshman. I loved having a boyfriend, a companion. Nothing else mattered when his arms were around me.

When Greg was at baseball practice, I'd climb through his bedroom window and fold his clothes, make the bed. He lived just down the block. I wrote him love letters and hid them in his shoes. He treated me well, too, with respect and pride, as we walked hand in hand through the halls of Taft High. I wore his flannel shirts, even to bed, where I missed him most—his breath hot on my neck, the way he would place my icy hands inside his shirt, warming them against his smooth chest. I thought I'd be with him forever.

And Greg had a car, which changed everything: a Datsun B210 with sheepskin-covered seats. The car, when not filled with marijuana smoke, smelled faintly of ashes and damp wool. We lived in our own world with the heater purring, the stereo bass vibrating our seats like a heartbeat. I no longer walked the rainy highway: he drove me to school, to and from work, and one weekend he taught me to drive.

Almost every day we'd park at a quiet beach access on the north part of town, at Road's End, where we could watch the sunset. We kissed and fumbled and traced each other's bodies with our fingers until the windows became opaque, until the ocean was something we heard only faintly. There in the bucket seats of his car, sweatshirts flung on the floor, we explored each other, our pale limbs tumbling. Often rain lashed the car, startling us, making us even more urgent, as if the world itself were about to lose control.

In the spring we made bonfires on the beach and leaned against logs, drinking his father's beers and counting the stars. We'd hold each other, listening to the ocean, and what I felt with him was wonderful not for its newness but for its familiarity. In those moments I returned to an intimacy I'd known long ago, as if what I had wanted all along was that feeling of refuge and comfort that I had known only those first months on Kauai, with my mother and father.

My teachers didn't approve of this union, but I didn't care. School was a social activity, as far as I was concerned. The science experiments and history lessons lost any significance outside class. Still, I liked my teachers, even Mr. Atkins, an earnest, lonely man who taught English. He desperately flung his enthusiasm at us, which we deflected with ease. I felt sorry for him, the way I would for a nightclub singer who was ignored by the crowd, and sometimes I gave him an apologetic wave as I left his class.

My mother accepted Greg, who was polite, charming, and got me home on time. But she didn't like that he was older. After two months she realized we were "serious," and one day she invited him over for a talk. The three of us sat in our living room, and my mother started it off.

"Now, Greg, I know you really like my daughter."

Greg, sitting two feet from me, nodded slightly, his ears red.

"And you're both teenagers, and I know that you'll want to have sex."

The word *sex* seemed to linger, the *x* fading in a slow hiss. Greg stared at his shoes. He always wore Nike sneakers with the giant swoosh along the sides, like everyone else. They had grease spots because his parents owned a service station.

"Well?"

What to answer? Greg and I had been screwing like rabbits for weeks. My mother waited. Greg gave an audible swallow that came out like an ambiguous grunt.

"I know it's true," she continued, and nodded at him reassuringly. "But I'd like you to know that you can't have sex with my daughter. She's too young. You can go out and have fun, but no sex. Do I have your agreement on this?"

Greg nodded.

"Okay, that's settled, then." She grinned, satisfied.

Greg and I left soon after to go to a party. I thought about my mother on the drive, how her words made no sense to me. Why would she deny me the pleasure of a man's arms? She knew, better than anyone, that I would find no warmer place.

Holding Patterns

I first met Brad, my mother's third husband, at their wedding. I was sixteen, and I didn't want to be there. I'd just returned from a year with my father and my brother Ken in Puget Sound, Washington. It was the first time I'd lived with my father, as kind of an experiment, to give my mother and me a break, and it hadn't gone well. I was tired, and raw, and I didn't want to join this new family that had sprung up like some strange garden while I was gone.

I was still reeling from what happened with my father. Alcoholic and jobless, he had hung on to his apartment with money sent from my mother and his mother. To cover the rest, he had an affair with the apartment manager, a gaudy, overweight redhead who wore blousy outfits and liked her drinks with lots of ice. He kept his involvement behind closed doors, but whenever I saw her around the property, I'd give her knowing looks. She ignored them.

We collected about seven pieces of furniture, including a couple of orange crates for tables and a plastic green and white lawn chair that served as a couch. My brother and I had our own rooms, but we split a bed between us—I took the mattress and left him with the box spring. I don't remember anything about my room except its squareness; it was a perfect, empty box. At night I'd lie on the mattress on the floor and stare at the ceiling, trying to find shapes and patterns.

Our apartment felt like a big waiting room, with my father camped out in one corner, surrounded by yellow legal pads, often drunk. He was finishing the book, *Gone to Maui,* that he'd been writing in Mill Valley. I knew he was a good writer, had been told so by people all my life. I'd saved all his letters to me, funny, wonderful stories from his daily life, complete with whole scenes of dialogue. They left me with a good feeling whenever I read them. But I couldn't shake the feeling that something was wrong. There was a connection between him and the drinking and the notepads, some mysterious triangle that he was locked in to and I was locked out of. We weren't nearly as close as we'd been during those weekends in Mill Valley. And Ken felt like a stranger. Part of that was my age. Now that I was fifteen and he was ten, we couldn't play together the way we had, those long days in the park. I'd no more dance with Ken for an audience than I'd take him along on a date—if I ever had one.

The three of us had some good times in the rec room, playing pool, but I took off whenever I could to spend the afternoons and evenings with Jenny, who lived in the apartment across the way. She introduced me to her friend Christy, a goofy, wild girl I took to immediately. Jenny, Christy, and I spent that August sizzling by the small apartment pool, slathered in Johnson's baby oil. We competed for the best tan, and eventually we turned as brown and sleek as the vinyl on the rec-room furniture, our palms and soles a pale pink. Later, we'd make cookies at Jenny's and share them with her plump, friendly mother, who never seemed to leave the place. They were like the people I'd known on the Oregon coast—earthy, irreverent, and, what I sensed but didn't know, they were lower middle class, like me.

As a new sophomore at Gig Harbor High, I encountered the first class system that directly affected me. The rich girls at school wore lovely clothes. I became aware of the significance of fabric: what cashmere meant. Angora. Silk. And their clothes looked brand-new. One girl in my French class whispered, as if telling me a secret, "You wore that shirt on Tuesday." Her sense of privilege and authority left me speechless. What's more, the shirt wasn't even mine (I'd become an expert at borrowing clothes from Jenny and Christy—my sparse wardrobe was pure hick).

The way I saw it, kids here lived like something out of *The Great Gatsby*. They skied in Canada and had birthday parties in Seattle. They lived in grand houses on the sound and, for birthdays, received cars and speedboats. I saw these houses from the inside only twice, when the party was big enough to allow overflow like me and Jenny and Christy. The most popular crowd was good-looking and athletic as well as rich, and the very air around them seemed to crackle with a celebratory recklessness. They could be and do and have anything they wanted.

In Lincoln City, everyone had been poor. My friends and I had all worked after-school jobs even before we could get legal work permits, and most parents waited tables, pumped gas, drove logging trucks. My mother worked and went to school, so we weren't any better off. That year with my father, though, I began to see that the world saw more than me—they saw where I came from and judged me for it.

I understood none of this back then. I saw myself through my classmates' eyes and wondered—a kind of self-torture—what they'd say if any of them ever caught a glimpse of our apartment. It was bad enough that my dad would sometimes pick me up in the car we'd gotten that fall, a rattling Buick with a smashed-in back left fender that gave the car a crippled look, as if we limped rather than rolled. Dad would pull up wearing a bored expression, flannel shirtsleeves pushed up, cigarette dangling from his mouth. He always carried a healthy disdain for snobs. It was one of the things he could have taught me if I had let him.

Sometimes I thought about Greg, my boyfriend from Lincoln City, but I didn't talk about him. He'd never answered my letters, and over the summer, he faded from my mind. This surprised me a little, but I'd gotten good at pushing away painful feelings, the way I'd look away from my father's blurry eyes. It was easier to focus on the boys around me than to think about Greg. I never told Jenny and Christy about him, and besides, they were saving themselves for marriage, so I pretended I was a virgin, too. And after a while I began to feel like one again. Although I had crushes on half a dozen boys, I dated only once in Gig Harbor, for three weeks, and it felt like I was holding my breath the whole time. Gary was a handsome, polite boy from a good family who went to church. He was one of the popular crowd, but I was cute enough to date, I knew that much. Just the girls gave him shit about me; the guys grinned or ignored us.

Gary took me for rides in his shiny car that smelled like new leather shoes. We'd neck in the back rows of movie theaters. But he never came to our apartment or took me out with his friends, and after a time of what must have felt to him like a double life, he stopped calling. I felt an almost physical pain for a week or so, and also a little relief. Everything about him suggested alternatives that I knew were closed to me.

By May my father's affair with the manager ended and she evicted us. I wasn't surprised when my mother arrived and pulled me out of school that day. My father, brother, and I had lived in a kind of holding pattern, not knowing how to land without crashing. Ken was sent on an airplane to his mother in Hawaii. When my mother walked in one day soon after, quickly glanced around our sparse apartment, and gathered me up in a shocked fury, I wanted to say, *It's not so bad.* But my loyalties were mixed.

My mother must have felt confused, too, for she knew my father was an alcoholic and couldn't hold a job, and she had let me live with him. This was an ambivalent rescue, and my mother and I drove back down to Oregon in a strained silence.

The wedding was held on a warm but windy day on the Oregon coast, at the Yaquina Bay Lighthouse high above the gray ocean that rippled toward a horizon hidden by clouds. I hoped this would be a good party, which to me meant boys and booze. But there were no prospects at the wedding, I saw that immediately. The pastor was ancient, my younger cousins pimply and unsophisticated. Alcohol was out, too, since both my mother and Brad had quit drinking. I was too self-absorbed to realize the miracle in this—my mother finding sobriety. Or maybe I just didn't trust it. Resigned to boredom, I took in the beauty of the place, the evergreens a velvety ribbon along the coast as far as I could see, the lighthouse stretching above us all like the neck of a giant white bird.

In the reception room, a table heaped with potluck fare—Swedish meatballs, a vegetable tray, vague, steamy dishes—sat in the center of the room. Relatives and friends huddled around it in the manner of chilled people around a fire, holding paper napkins and cups of punch, exchanging well-meaning smiles. In the corner, the cake rose in gaudy white tiers. Later, we sat outside and ate slices of that fluffy cake while seagulls soared above us.

There was an odd mood all day. It was as if the guests were trying to muster the energy for one more cheer for a losing team. The whole time I avoided my mother, who was excited and teary-eyed. She was too busy to notice that I kept wandering off. I felt very distant from her, and I knew enough to stay clear during these moods of hers, to avoid an emotional embrace or crying jag. I can't even remember what she was wearing—I keep seeing the green ensemble from her wedding to Steve years later, on a beach about sixty miles north. The guests, too, blur from one wedding to the next.

Instead of watching her, I watched the groom from afar. My new stepfather. He was twenty-six, and my mother thirty-nine. This was significant. Gorgeous Joe from Lincoln City had been twenty-one, and that relationship hadn't lasted long. Less important but to me another oddity was Brad's height: he was shorter than my mother by at least an inch. I believed men should be taller than women. These facts put them off balance in my mind from the start.

I studied Brad, trying to get a read from his appearance. I'd gotten good at that over the years. He walked with a bounce, hands in his pockets in an aw-shucks sort of way. A lot of brown curly hair sprouted from various places, and this manly luxuriance seemed to contrast with his tidy round glasses. His glossy mustache, thick as a pickle, curled over his upper lip, and I thought: *How in the world are they going to kiss with that thing in the way?* My father never had a mustache, or Mac, either, but Tom had. This seemed a bad sign. I later discovered with distaste that Brad groomed it daily with a fancy set of brushes, clippers, and oils. I tried to decide if he was good-looking and concluded he was about average. Maybe the most interesting thing about him was a nervous tic—every few moments he'd glance around and then blink fiercely, as if baffled by the situation he found himself in.

I distanced myself from the entire affair, but I couldn't resist the romance of the day, even if I applied it only to myself. I looked in the bathroom mirror, loving the off-white dress I wore, my bare and tan shoulders. At one point I walked alone to the cliff and stood gazing out at the sea, feeling sorry for myself, imagining that the highway travelers thought me a lonely bride.

We moved to Portland so my mother and Brad could go to school—she for her master's in social work and he for certification as a paramedic. Financially, things were almost as bad as they'd been with my father. We rented the first of three houses and took in two boarders, Mary Beth and Dale, to help out. Mary Beth was short and wore her red hair long and wild; it billowed around her face like a curtain. She lived up to that hair, swearing and laughing loudly, throwing her weight around like a sailor. Dale, a shy young man, lived off the kitchen in a small room, and I was curious about his habits.

One day, snooping in his room, I discovered a pile of pornography in his closet—slick, shocking magazines stacked high as my hips. This completely unnerved me, and glancing through a few of them, I felt dizzy, sickened, and vaguely aroused. He was such a nice man, I thought. I watched him closely but stayed aloof, and from then on the house seemed even more like someone else's, a place that would never be my home.

My mother and Brad were inventive, clipping coupons and searching out bargain deals. We bought in bulk, shared clothes, reused jars and bags. I took care of most of my own needs through my jobs at Dairy Queen and then the Gap, jobs I felt both grateful for and burdened by. To feed all of us, including Mary Beth and Dale, we baked bread on a schedule overseen by Brad—dozens of stout brown loaves that left the kitchen steamy and moist twice a week. On the counter, a Crock-Pot of beans simmered nearly every night, and the rich, loamy smell of chili permeated the rooms and our clothes. We lived like pioneers in the middle of the city, which gave us all a hardy but desperate quality.

My brother Dace was still in elementary school, and we steered clear of each other, mainly because we had so little in common. For a year he made my mother crazy by insisting on sleeping under his bed. Every night he built a barrier of stuffed animals that stood facing outward from around the bed's base like pleasant sentries. She pleaded with him to leave an air hole, and he agreed. He would say good night through it, his round face peeking out from between bears.

At least Dace got along with Brad. I didn't. Brad liked to give orders and set limits, as in *My brush is off limits to you kids.* He was recently out of the army and liked things clean and organized. I'd leave hair in the bathroom, clumps of toothpaste congealing on the counter. I forgot my clothes in the washer and they'd start to stink. He was most fanatical about food and cleanliness, though all of my habits disgusted him.

But he also had an ebullient sense of fun. He sang joyously in the shower, twirled my laughing mother around the kitchen, pulled out a cute Texas accent like a magic trick from a hat. I'd often come across him holding her tight, whispering in her ear, making her laugh. He had many talents that demonstrated his resourcefulness: he could juggle fruit and cans of soup, and he could draw. Wonderful cartoon characters papered the refrigerator. My mother adored him.

His most annoying trick was the Spaniel. He'd attach white sweatsocks to his ears so they draped like floppy ears, and then he'd crawl around on all fours, panting happily, then jumping up on the bed to lap my mother's chin while she laughed hysterically. She loved this, and I'd sometimes hear her say, "Oh, please, do the Spaniel."

I looked on all of this with the disdain of one who wants to join in but doesn't know how. This pissed off Brad, who called me the "ice queen" and a "cadaver," because he said I reminded him of the bodies in his anatomy class. I was afraid of Brad's fierce, jolly approach to life. I overheard him time and again pleading to my mother, *"What's her problem?"* Over that year he gave up on me and began to use his cheerfulness like a prod, exposing my sullen pride.

At school I was miserable. I'd enrolled in my third high school in three years, a giant institution with blocks of lockers and dozens of halls that I wandered forlornly. Even though I'd left friends and schools many times before, I missed Jenny and Christy with an urgency I hadn't expected and had no way to deal with. I avoided the cavernous cafeteria for weeks, its throngs of ruthless, laughing teenagers. Instead, I'd eat my lunch perched on the toilets in bathroom stalls and then escape to read in the library for the rest of the lunch hour. I knew this was weird, embarrassing behavior, and I never told anyone, least of all my mother and Brad.

After about a month I became friendly with a girl who lived down the street and rode the same bus to school. Her name was Ann Booth, and she was cruelly confident, with lovely skin and absolutely perfect clothes. Sometimes she invited me over after school and we'd experiment with makeup. I coveted her white turtlenecks with their patterns of little skiers and evergreen trees, and her collection of Izod shirts in a rainbow of colors. I carefully rehearsed how I'd ask to borrow a shirt, achieving just the right tone of nonchalance. Ann wasn't as forgiving as Jenny, though, and would change her mind at the last minute or require me to say "pretty please." At school she treated me like an acquaintance.

I began to skip school whenever I could; I picked my days according to Brad's overnight work schedule, when I knew he'd be gone. The hostility between us was only getting worse. One day I came home to the blessed solitude of the house. I made a sandwich, planning to clean up later, and took it to my room. Then, to my horror, I heard someone come in the house. Brad's voice called out and my stomach dropped. On instinct, I hid in my closet. Then, silence. I pictured him in the kitchen surveying my mess: the crumbs, the mayonnaise jar open to bacteria, the leftover bread already going stale. The waste! He swore bitterly and stomped down the hall toward my room, almost at a run. He knew no one else would so flagrantly break the rules. Terrified, I froze. He came into my room and strode about, breathing heavily—looking for something to break or smash, I imagined. I could see him through a crack as he passed back and forth like a bear in a cage. I held my breath, sure he could hear my heart beat. God, what if he checked the closet! Then he picked up my curling iron from the dresser and slashed the air in quick, sweeping arcs.

I doubted he would hurt me physically; what worried me was discovery. My cowardice would be revealed, I'd be ridiculed by him forever. And what if he was exposed in the midst of this fit? The image of him fencing the air with my pink curling iron would have had me howling with laughter if I hadn't been so scared. Then he stopped his slashing and put the iron down, and looked at himself in the mirror for a long moment before he left. It seemed he was almost about to speak, and sometimes, even now, I wonder what he would have said.

Romance

In my junior year I went to Hawaii for spring break, to see my father. He was living in Waikiki in a cheap hotel room with my brother Ken and a twenty-one-year-old tourist from Kentucky. Her name was Brandy, and she had ditched her friends to stay with my father. A few days before I arrived, I learned later, my father had come back to their hotel room and found it padlocked; all their stuff, even my brother's schoolbooks, had been impounded. They never did get it back.

He was trying to finish his book, and he was almost done. There was no more money to borrow from friends or family or the bank, so he had started house-sitting, spending a few days in apartments and cottages, watering plants and feeding cats.

My father and brother picked me up at the airport. My father gave me a big hug, and I could tell he was glad to see me. Then I saw a girl off to the side, smiling and holding a lei. She looked about eighteen or nineteen and wore a tank top and miniskirt over her rubbery puppylike body. Her pert nose was sunburned, freckles like thrown paint over her nose. She wore her sunglasses pushed up to hold back her curly mess of brown hair. I didn't think she was very pretty, but she was sort of cute in a Shirley Temple kind of way. This was Brandy, my father told me after he hugged me.

I wasn't expecting her, though she was expecting me, and I felt that put her at an unfair advantage. But she seemed happy to meet me—she had made the plumeria lei for me and gave me a kiss as she draped it over my neck. Right away she started describing the apartment my father had scored for two weeks in Makiki, on the edge of Honolulu. It had nice furniture and *lauhala* mats on the floors. There were two bedrooms, one for my brother and the other for my father and Brandy, and I could sleep on a couch in the living room.

We loaded my suitcase in the trunk and headed toward Honolulu. My father was quiet as he drove, smoking, while Brandy chattered on. There was an awkward silence, and then my father said he had a joke for me, and that got us all started, so on the drive back to the apartment we told jokes and laughed all the way.

Brandy announced that I needed a tan, and I did. I looked like what I was: a mainland haole just off the plane. So we prepared for a day at the beach. Brandy thrust her stubby body into a hot-pink bikini that matched her hot-pink fingernails, as she pointed out, and she let me borrow a sarong to wrap over my blue one-piece suit. She advised me to put my hair up, like hers, which she had gathered in a coco-palm topknot, genie-style, with corkscrew curls springing out like distress signals. We stood side by side in front of the mirror and saw that we were opposites—I was almost five inches taller, blond, and skinny. My father poked his head in the door then and chuckled, and I realized how silly we must have looked to him, but Brandy strutted around like a model. I could tell she had no shame.

As we ran out the door to catch the bus, my father told us to have fun. At the beach we laid out our towels and sodas and magazines near the pink Royal Hawaiian Hotel, right in the middle of Waikiki Beach, with what seemed like a million other people. We splayed out under the sun and sizzled our innocent skin, checking the progress of our tan lines every fifteen minutes by peeling our suits back an inch. Then we'd exchange encouraging remarks like "Wow, it's way darker now."

Brandy didn't tan so well, just turned a ruddy pink, and her freckles stood out like a thousand tiny stop signs. By three o'clock I was sunburned, not too bad, but enough so that my body would radiate heat steady as a woodstove all night long. To cool off, Brandy went to the snack bar and got us some shave ice, a kind of Popsicle in a cone, and we sucked on them until our mouths turned bright, wild colors. As we lay there, she told me all about her goals in life. She was going into the army in a year or so, where she would drive tanks and wear camouflage outfits. Later, after the army, she would get married and have lots of kids, at least five, but she didn't say if she wanted my father to be the husband. I couldn't see it, and I definitely didn't want to.

I just listened while the Oregon weather, which had dug itself deep into my pores, evaporated off my body in a slow steam. Brad was a million miles away. I pictured him frozen and wet in Portland, and smiled.

Brandy and I had oiled ourselves so thoroughly that sand stuck to us in smooth patches whenever we strayed beyond the safety of our beach towels. "Damn," she'd say, and try to rub it off. I kept checking out her body from behind my sunglasses. Her tight suit pressed into her flesh, which swelled over the sides. I thought, *My father has sex with this body.* I never would have looked at a woman my father's age this way. Every half hour or so a guy would make his way over to us and squat down by our towels. They asked a lot of questions: whether we were tourists, whether we were single, if we had a hotel room, if we enjoyed partying. We were always incredibly flattered by this attention, even though the guys would stop at some other girl's towel down the beach every time.

We didn't make a date with any of them. We treated it as a game, but still, the whole thing was a little embarrassing. There was no way I was going to ask Brandy about my dad. We didn't talk about him. I asked only where they met, which she told me was at the Tahitian Lanai, the Hilton's poolside bar, my father's hangout. There was the lingering sense that something was wrong; it was like listening to a slightly off-key song. I daydreamed to take my mind off it. When I lay on my stomach, I could see between the great towers of the hotels and office buildings to the island's mountains beyond, lush and green, as if they were underwater. My father had taken me to that side of the island many times; my uncle and cousins lived over there. Clouds clung to the mountaintops, where I could tell it was raining. Though it was too far to see, I knew there were also waterfalls and rainbows.

And when I turned around, there was the beach under a bleached blue sky, and it was glorious. Everyone looked beautiful if I squinted my eyes, sleeping beauties sprawled everywhere like confetti-colored sprinkles on a golden cake, and I lay there amazed at my presence on this tropical island in the middle of the ocean. Except for the times in Mill Valley and Washington, I'd always come to Hawaii to see my father, but it seemed I was just beginning to appreciate it as unique from places on the mainland. Everything seems equally amazing when you're a child, but as you get older, it takes more to make you stop and shiver with wonder.

We and everyone around us glittered and the sun poured itself over us, holding nothing back, a firey love holding us in a profound embrace.

My father spent his days writing at the Tahitian Lanai, where it was dim and quiet, hidden by enormous palm fronds and the thatched walls and roof of the bar. This was a secluded oasis from the chaos of Waikiki. Because you couldn't see them, you could forget about the Hilton's two skyscrapers looming above the tiny bar. Waitresses with long, smooth sheets of hair and names like Malia and Lani and Crystal served strong drinks. My father didn't have a job—he was hoping that his book, self-published with friends he'd known in school at Punahou, would do well. It was coming out soon. What better place to wait? The Tahitian Lanai had been around for a long time, had a history, and locals seemed to like it more than tourists. A scuffed black Steinway piano sat in one corner of the bar, and now and then someone would play some old songs and a few people would gather around and sing.

This was the place that brought my father and this girl together. I've often tried to imagine it: my father sits at the bar with a Budweiser, smoking a cigarette, taking a break from the writing. He's in his early forties, sandy blond and tall, with a belly tucked away under his aloha shirt. Faded jeans, topsiders. His face is handsome enough so you almost ignore the damage from drinking and smoking, the watery eyes. People still tell him he looks like Steve McQueen and, once in a while, Robert Redford.

She comes in with two friends, giggly and sandy from the beach. She's cute, but it's mostly her youth that is attractive. She's just twenty-one, so the colorful drinks appeal to her, the ones with rum and fruit juice and pineapple slices.

She hoists her fetching plump butt onto the bar stool. It could have been any one of them, but she sits closest to my father. My father is interested in their presence, their chatter. It's as if three large parrots have alighted there at the bar. He listens as a writer listens, and at a certain point he deftly enters the conversation, offers something funny or useful. Maybe Brandy is looking for sandals or wants to know if pedicab drivers will rip you off. He makes her feel like a woman, like an adult, but he still lets her know that he has a substantial store of wisdom that she might benefit from. He knows which beaches to go to, where to find a good cheap breakfast.

She's impressed at the way he buys them a round, as if it were nothing, and then she notices his green eyes. He says, "I'll be here tomorrow about this time."

Most of all she likes how he makes her laugh. How he makes her feel special.

After the beach Brandy took me into the bedroom and taught me to dance sexy, told me that it was all about the hips and knees. She told me to think about roller skating, which I was pretty good at. Bend and dip and keep your body smooth-not-stiff. Her body shone in the late-afternoon sun streaming through the window. She turned up the music and gyrated. My father, trying to watch the news, told us to pipe down, but she ignored him. I had begun to realize that I didn't especially like Brandy. She didn't have any class that I could see, but I was a little in awe of her. Brandy seemed like a grown woman to me. She seemed to know exactly what she was doing all the time, whether it was ordering from the beach snack bar or planning to enter the army.

As far as my father was concerned, I'd last seen him in Washington, lonely and tired. I wasn't sure why he was with Brandy, because she was kind of embarrassing, and my father hated to be embarrassed. I didn't understand him, but I assumed she didn't mind his drinking and didn't tell him what to do. I watched him with Ken, who wasn't around much. I vaguely knew that things had happened between my father and my brother since our year together in Washington. They seemed both closer and farther apart. Ken was only twelve years old, but sometimes I believed he knew more than I did about life. I knew something was wrong here, with this "family," this "girlfriend," this house we were staying in that was somebody else's. I suspected that my father didn't know what he was doing, that no one was in charge. But by sixteen I'd become very good at taking reality and turning it just slightly so that it was seen at another, more pleasant angle—like a kaleidoscope. I could do this as long as I had to. That is how I got through those few days, by shifting the truth in my mind, by seeing what I wanted to see.

So I figured she was fun for him, for a while. She always wore tight shirts that showed her belly, a round soft place that my dad pinched and patted to hear her giggle. They liked to make each other laugh. Watching them together, I tried to imagine Brandy as my stepmother, as the mother of a new little brother or sister. It was a strange idea. But even now I think: Who can say what is right and what is not for someone else?

The dancing lessons were a success, and Brandy announced that we were going out on the town, just us girls. My father wouldn't have gone anyway; he wasn't into nightlife. He liked to read and watch TV and avoid the crowds, and he always went to bed fairly early. He suggested a few places we should check out. When I finally came out of the bathroom, he pushed a ten-dollar bill in my hand. "Be good," he said.

We were all dolled up and paraded around for my father, who sat on the couch with his beer, smoking a cigarette. He seemed amused and maybe bored. If he was hurt, and I doubt he was, he wouldn't have shown it. Of course I don't know what he was thinking that night, but I suspect he was glad to be rid of us, of our nervous anticipation, our young hormones bubbling over like cheap champagne. Do you think he knew what we were up to? Did he know about all the young guys everywhere, like the kind we'd seen on the beach that day? Of course he did. Sometimes I felt my father could see all the way into the pit of my heart and still he loved me.

As we walked to the bus, I told Brandy, "Dad gave me ten dollars."

Annoyingly, he had given her money, too. She showed me a twenty folded in her coin purse.

"Listen," she said. "We won't have to pay for shit if we're smart. That's the way it works: you get a guy to pick up your tab."

She told me about the marine who had sent a whole bottle of white wine to her table. She'd had entire dinners picked up. Even my father had done it for her. But I wasn't sure I liked the idea— what if the guy was some kind of creep? I decided not to worry about it. We waited for the bus at sunset, and the color spread over the sky in the exact orange of the shave ice I'd had that day. I was ready for glamour, though it was clear at once that the bus was not glamorous but gross. It wheezed and lurched along, spewing out plumes of exhaust as we passed through neighborhoods where whole families lived in sweltering one-bedroom apartments. Clothes hung drying on rusty banisters, little kids sat on concrete stairs this close to the busy street.

Brandy checked her makeup in her compact, clownish in the fluorescent light. A grimy mixture of sand and sticky substances had attached to the floor and the soles of our sandals. We were ignored by older Japanese women clutching sacks of fruit and strange groceries, and watched by oily-looking men from the corners of their eyes. Out the window, I spied a red convertible full of joyous tourist girls rolling by, their blond hair blowing like wheat in the wind.

But between buildings, I caught glimpses of Waikiki curving along the ocean, glittering and sparkling before us in the twilight like Christmas, like a pinball machine we were ready to shoot ourselves into. I felt a wave of excitement ripple through me. We got off on Kuhio Avenue, and we walked the length of it while Brandy pointed out the transvestites with their lovely brown legs and shiny lips. We passed local boys leaning against palm trees, selling marijuana. They'd hiss at us, *"Hey, you like smoke?"*

I wasn't aware of it then, but there are parts of this island that normal, respectable tourists, like those from the Midwest, don't ever see. Korean bars tucked into alleys where the women do things I still can't believe. Massage parlors and opium dens—and in the jungles, people crawl out of steamy huts to pit roosters against each other for fortunes. It created an undercurrent of lust and greed that I could feel around me but couldn't explain.

I don't remember all the places we went. They're probably gone now. All I do remember is that they seemed the same—in each we breathed humid air laced with cigarette smoke and the scents of outrageous flowers, and we were surrounded by surfing memorabilia, tiki torches, the tropical decorations that cover every establishment in the islands—as if people didn't know they were on an island in the middle of the Pacific and needed constant reminding. What did we discuss in those lounges and bars over candlelight? As bizarre and silly as our talk must have been, I wish I could hear it now. Sometimes I get the feeling that if I could hear one conversation from my past, things today would make more sense.

We had a hard time getting into dance clubs because I didn't have an ID, which was embarrassing to me and pissed off Brandy. When I was barred from the Wave, Brandy called them assholes and danced just outside the door while the bouncers eyed her carefully, the way one might watch a child who was on the verge of destroying something. Restaurants were easier. The drinking age was still eighteen then, and besides, we only went to places with male bartenders, so Brandy could flirt with them. She called me her "daughter" all night, which always made us laugh, since I was taller and more subdued and she didn't look much older.

She'd done this before, left my father and gone out dancing and looking for younger men. So why was she with him? It wasn't for his money, because he really didn't have any, though he did provide free rent. Maybe for a girl like Brandy this might be exciting, living with an older man on a tropical island. She didn't read books, she hadn't been to college—what did she know? And she didn't look much past the surface of things, I noticed. Take the way she saw maraschino cherries: to me they were fake, dyed, and sickly sweet; but she liked them because they tasted good, and that was all that mattered. She'd eat two and three at a time, scooping a handful as we passed the cocktail-waitress section.

But my father was sweet and funny and gentle. He'd tear up at sad movies or when a certain song came on, something that made him nostalgic, like "Honolulu City Lights." He was never mean. Even though he was smart enough to expose a person's weakest points, he never did. In fact, he'd defend people I made fun of. I think he was aware that he had plenty of his own flaws, and that it was simply bad form to point out those in others. He was a deeply kind person. That's one of the things I loved best about him.

We ended up at the Chart House, down by the marina, a place with dim lighting and the smell of steak in the air. It was there that we met two European men who bought us food because we were starving and flat broke by then. We had piña coladas for dessert. The men were older, maybe even in their thirties, and from somewhere in the Mediterranean. When the flower girl came by draped with leis and cut roses, the men bought us each a carnation lei. This seemed a true romantic gesture, and as they presented them to us with a kiss, it felt as significant as if they'd bought us rings. I could tell Brandy was impressed—she had said earlier that day that European men were the best, but I didn't know at what. She kept looking at me and raising her eyebrows, as if to make sure I was aware of our good luck.

Now and then I thought of my father at home. I'd think, *He's probably watching TV* or *He's asleep by now,* but I never shared these thoughts with Brandy. It seemed impolite, like reminding a person that she's doing something wrong and that you're a part of it, too.

One of the men began paying extra attention to Brandy, and the other settled on me. His heavy accent made our conversation funny at first, and then just slow and unnerving. His hands were long and brown and slender, and they reminded me of spiders in the candle-light. But he had a pleasant face. The silk of his shirt shimmered in the lights. He was like something out of *Saturday Night Fever,* which had been one of my favorite movies.

The men had a hotel room nearby and invited us back for a drink and to see their view. It must have been after midnight by the time we went there with them. They had a nice room with an adjoining bedroom and Hawaiian music playing on the radio. I was fairly drunk, and the memories seemed blurred to me now, as if seen through fog, but what remains most clear is standing with my "date" on the hotel lanai that overlooked the swimming pool far below. I thought, *Wow, we're sixteen stories high, and I'm sixteen.* I also saw that he had taken off his shoes, which irritated me. I didn't like that I could see his naked feet with their tendons and patches of hair. It was a strange intimacy and seemed to suggest that this was just the beginning.

The other thing I remember is the wind swirling my skirt up, but it was really his hand, his dark hand, and far below, the pool glowed blue and clear as a mirror. I could just see my reflection.

I wasn't a virgin, but it had been a long time since I had even kissed a boy—not since Washington the year before. And I'd never been romantic with a grown man. Fear washed over me with a suddenness that turned me cold. My stomach was upset, full of beef and coconut milk and liquor, and I thought I might be sick. I decided I wanted to go home very badly.

I went inside to find Brandy, but she was behind the bedroom door, and it was quiet in there. I knocked, and knocked again, and I heard something like "Just a minute." It was a long time before she came out. I waited in strained silence with the barefoot man, who seemed depressed. When Brandy opened the door, I saw that she still had her lei on, but it was wilted, and gaps of dirty string showed between the flowers. She didn't look at me, but it was clear she was annoyed and that she'd just put on lipstick, though not carefully.

Brandy and I walked home, all the way to Makiki, through misty veils of rain drifting from deep in the valleys on their way to the sea. We didn't talk much; what was there to say? When we got home, it was starting to get light, the world's eyelid lifting ever so slightly, revealing the sweetest pink, like you'd find in a seashell.

We tiptoed in, and we were quiet as clouds, so as not to wake my father.

13

The Place Between Them

In the fall of my senior year, my mother came into my room and sat carefully on the bed. I was ready. This was how we always faced tough times: someone has to go. What I didn't realize was that this time it would be me. She very gently asked me if I wouldn't like to go live in Hawaii with my father, who had gotten engaged to a lawyer, a woman his age. The idea surprised me. It seemed to me that we'd been through that only a year and half before, in Washington. But things were different now, she said. This new woman was successful and very responsible. Brandy was long gone. Dad had gotten it together, was cutting down on the drinking. They were even considering buying a house. And Hawaii! I loved Hawaii, didn't I? Her words were animated, but her body was stiff, and she looked about to cry.

I had the sensation of movement, as if I were already on the airplane, taking off. I thought of the flight over the ocean, traveling from my mother to my father. What was there in that place between them?

I kept quiet and still, hugging my knees. As long as I was still, I wouldn't follow the motion that was already in place. Inside, though, I felt like I was on fire. Had she forgotten that my father drank daily, that we'd lived like squatters, eating chili from the can and hot dogs and iceberg lettuce six nights a week? Had she chosen Brad over me? Did she realize that after this I'd go to college, that this was it? I thought of the wonderful friends I'd made at school, finally, Erin and Molly and crazy Careena, of our late nights over cheap coffee at the diner, our day trips to the coast to see the ocean. I'd be leaving them, too.

But I then thought of Hawaii, picturing the envy on my classmates' and teachers' faces when I told them the news. I'd leave the wet gloom of Portland, take off on a shiny white plane, and learn to surf and hula dance in the islands. I'd go to a Hawaiian high school and eat papayas and mangoes every morning for breakfast. I would see Ken again, get to know him better now that we were a little older. My grandmother was there, and my four cousins I used to play with in the summers. And maybe my father would be different in Hawaii, sweet and content, the way I remembered him from Mill Valley.

I told her what she wanted to hear: I said okay. It comes down to a matter of perspective in the end—either you decide to leave, or someone tells you to go. I wasn't trying to make peace, I just realized that the decision was neither her doing nor my choice: it was the natural course of things.

Only now do I realize that at seventeen I had become like my mother—I had started my own pattern of leaving and starting over. She had taught me how to leave. What I never learned, and maybe never will, is how to stay.

14

This Is What It Means
to Be a Daughter

My fathers, in chronological order: Ken, Michael, Mac, Tom, Brad, and Steve. That's how I keep track—I put them in order. There were some in between who stayed around for a few months or even a year, but I don't count them. I count only the ones who changed me in some way, better or worse, and it doesn't matter whether my mother married them as long as they considered me a daughter.

At some point I began to see my past in something like eras—like a country's succession of kings—as in "The Mac Period" or "The Tom Years." Sometimes the fathers overlapped and I had to swiftly adjust. I got used to watching men leave, but in the end it doesn't matter who left who. There's just the leaving, and what is left afterward.

I wondered at other kids who'd always had the same father. I studied their dads. I watched TV shows featuring the wise, kind fathers who never leave, like *The Waltons, Little House on the Prairie,* and *Happy Days.* In the beginning these shows seemed full of miracles, though by junior high, I realized they weren't real. But I never missed a show.

Nearly always a new father meant a hasty move to a new house or town, which often required a new school. This was sometimes a good thing; I could start over, again and again. Of course I lost friends, some of whom I missed for a long time, and even today I remember their names, see their faces.

It became natural by the fourth or fifth father to withdraw a bit, keep my distance. This was wise because of the new rules and habits to adapt to. Some fathers let me jump on the bed; others watched to make sure I made it properly. The older I got, the smarter I felt. I believed I was superior to the new man, that I knew something he didn't. I placed bets with Dace on how long the guy would stick around, and we'd compete to see who could do the best imitation of him.

All along I kept in mind that I had a "real" father somewhere— my blood father. This was important, and some dads, when they left, took advantage of that distinction to ease the fact of their leaving. They'd say, "I'm not going to be around anymore, but don't forget, your real father will always be there."

And years later, when my real father is dying—too early, before I'm ready—under the pain will be what feels like panic. I've always been told he was there somewhere, that no matter who was coming and going, my real father was *always there*. This knowledge is part of me, gives me comfort, and what will I do when he's gone?

Living with different fathers became its own kind of school, the trick being to figure out which lesson to go with. My mother did the leaving most often, and I learned from her how to tend to my happiness: I began to understand that the best way out of a bad choice is the door. I also learned that every man has a breaking point, and that it could take the form of yelling or crying or a mean silence. Sometimes a man broke windows or dishes, and sometimes he directed that rage at my mother, or at me and my brother.

Despite the difficulty that only a man can bring, it's also true that life is hard and disappointing *without* a man. My mother became even harder to reach. Her contentment was a mystery to us—fleeting and elusive. I knew I could never provide it for her, knew it could be found only in association with a man. It was understood that I and my mother and my brother were incomplete in the between-men times.

Early on, I decided that it is always better to have a man around.

. . .

This is what it means to be a daughter: you're a package deal. I came with the mother, not the other way around, and each man treated me accordingly. I was accepted or resented and often a combination of the two. Trust became something hard to hold on to, harder to hold than air, than water.

There was no pattern. I didn't see much difference between living together and marriage. My fathers didn't look or smell or sound alike. Some of them I loved; others I hated and hid from. There was only change. Change is the most familiar aspect of my life: I have lived always with restlessness.

No matter how they distinguished themselves in my mind, their differences never overrode the common truth of them: each man eventually left, and another took his place.

A man was my father for a few years, and he wiped my nose and taught me his favorite songs or told me about Orion or read to me from books about Alaska. But I never saw any of them again. That was the hardest part, even if I didn't like them much. The truth is, I gave pieces of my childhood to these men. What if I could see them all in one room? I would ask each in turn: *What is one thing you remember about me?*

I tell myself they loved me and they haven't forgotten me. I'll believe it as long as I can.

Island Girl

For a while I have the hill to myself, and the only sounds are the rustle of the plumeria tree leaves above me and the *purr-purr* of the gray doves in the grass. The bus is late. Just beyond, at the high school, classes haven't let out for lunch yet, and the campus seems abandoned. I want to sleep here on this hill above the city, in the shade, away from everyone.

Before long a boy, a little older, maybe nineteen, comes strolling slowly around the corner. He seems to be wandering with no place to be. Then he sees me and veers my way, begins climbing the slope. He sits down beside me, too close. There's something wrong with him. He should be in school or at work, and he smiles too much, his eyes invisible behind the black wall of his sunglasses, the wrap-around kind. Like two tiny white moons, my face is caught in their reflection.

"Eh, sistah," he says.

"Hi," I say quietly, and look at the books in my lap, the one for Hawaiian history class and *Brave New World,* which I'm reading for senior English. These are the only classes I need to graduate, and I'm glad I can take them in the morning and leave before lunch, because lunchtime is hell.

Beside me he is nearly naked, his shorts and plastic slippers all he needs in the heat. Wavy and slick, his hair is reddish in the sun. He wears a necklace of cowrie shells, has the strong shoulders of a surfer, like my brother. Like the other local boys, his skin is smooth and hairless except for the sparse black tangles low on his calves. I'm fish-belly white next to his brown body, with its perfect surface, free of the smallest freckle or spot. The blond hairs of my arms bristle in the trade winds.

The walk is so long to the school office, to the nearest classroom. Even the bathroom is no escape because the Samoan girls will be there, and they told me they'd kill me if they could.

Above us, the plumeria tree whispers and offers a shade that shifts in the wind, and the petals of its flowers scattered on the ground are spotted and curled. Small amber cockroaches burrow in the spiky grass at our feet. His toes are brown, but the undersides are pale and soft-looking, and that is the only fragile part of him that I can see.

He slides closer to me, daring, smiling. He makes comments, but the words tumble and I can't pin them down. He's speaking pidgin English, like the other kids and even some of the teachers. I say, "What?" to be polite, and he repeats himself, but it won't help. Even if he speaks slowly, I don't know the slang, and then I really am the *stupid haole* they're all calling me in the halls.

He laughs, but it's a curious laugh. He can't place me—I'm not a local haole and I'm not a tourist, and without an identity, I become for him, maybe, a victim. He looks at me the way the other kids do, even the other white kids—I've seen only five out of a few hundred students. All the kids look me up and down and laugh. Even as I hate them, I envy them.

I clutch the bottom of my dress to my legs, watching for the cockroaches. There is no one around. The cinder-block neighborhood houses crouch empty and hidden behind monkeypod trees and small palms, and awnings slant like lowered hat brims over their doors. Who would hear me? And who would understand me anyway, when I don't know the language?

The sun hangs full in the sky, the day shines bright and heavy and hot. It's February, and I've been on an island in the middle of the sea for almost two weeks.

This is his hill, and I envy his comfort. He asks me if I have a boyfriend and I say yes, though it's a lie, and he seems to know it. I move my legs to the right a little bit so we're not so close, so I won't encourage him, but carefully, so as not to offend him, either. It's hard to ignore his odd confidence, the sly grin. Maybe if I keep denying his unspoken threat, he won't carry it out. The bus will come soon.

On the other side of the island, my father is probably napping in his new house, a library book propped open on his chest. His fiancée sits at her desk at her law office in downtown Honolulu. I've known her just over a week—their wedding is days away. What would I say if I called her? Though I'll discover later she has a tender heart, so far she's been a busy, brisk woman who expects me to face life with confident efficiency. She'd probably say, "Tell him to get lost." She's told me I'll make friends, that I have to be patient.

And in the past I always have, eventually. But this is my fourth high school. And this time I can't blend into the crowd until I get my bearings. My clothes from Oregon are all wrong, and the few island-style clothes I've bought just make me stand out even more. I'm tall and awkward and blond, my shoulders sunburned raw pink. Even if I could, I wouldn't call my father or my soon-to-be stepmother. I don't want to be a problem, to rock the new marriage with my small troubles.

Really, there is nothing to do but wait.

The boy plucks at the hem of my sundress, which stretches just over my knees. It's brand-new, thin cotton with bright blue hibiscus flowers.

"You one island girl, eh?" he asks, and laughs.

I pull into myself and look away from him in the direction of the bus. There's no going back. I won't let him or anyone scare me away. This is where I live now. This is my home.

16

Exposure

It could have been anyone's fantasy, I admit. Our idea was to take pictures of one another and give them to our boyfriends. A Valentine's present. Richelle and Susan and I gathered rolls of film and champagne one of us had gotten as a present, as well as lingerie, sundresses, and bathing suits, whatever we could find, even scarves and robes and high-heeled shoes in different colors.

We didn't know where to go, but we knew we needed a private place. Our dorm rooms wouldn't work, not the beach or park. I thought of my father's house, which would be empty until late in the evening—I knew he and his wife had gone to Maui for the day. Surrounded and shaded by trees and ferns, cool and quiet, it was perfect. They lived less than a mile from campus in Manoa Valley, where houses sat on the swell of the valley's rise like small white boats on a wave. During college I rode my bike to their house once a week, laundry stuffed in a pack, and read long books on their lanai, next to the banana tree that rippled in the trade winds, a white cat named Palaka asleep beside me. While my stepmother was at work, my father would help me with my papers, or tell me stories, or we'd just sit quietly together and read. Of all the houses I've known, I miss that one the most.

. . .

When we got there, we were embarrassed, laughing nervously as we chose our outfits and loaded the film. At first we struck magazine poses, images of what we thought meant desire. We showed our "best sides" and held our stomachs in. I took pictures of Susan, a miniature inside the viewfinder. She lay curved like a cat on the couch, in a cream-colored nightgown, brown hair long and loose, lips dark as berries. This was how she wanted to be seen. "David will like this," she said, and looked at me like I was David, like she wanted me. I focused in, then out, and felt like I was holding her in my hands.

Richelle took my pictures while Susan helped, arranging a hem, fixing a strap, brushing away a strand of hair. In one I stand wearing only jeans, my back to the camera. I look over my shoulder at the floor, face in profile, my back a fragile *V.* In another I wear a cotton robe while sitting at the breakfast table, my hair up in a knot. I've put on Richelle's glasses, and one of my father's books lies open in my lap. I look up at the camera in what I believe to be sexy intellectualism.

In some I stand against the lanai railing, framed by the banana tree and its giant fronds. My dress is long and white, and I have on black heels, which show scuffs if you look closely enough. I wanted, I suppose, to feel what it would be like to be different women. Later, I leaned against my father's dresser in a black-and-white sundress. "Smile," Richelle said, and then she asked if I loved him, and she meant my boyfriend, Jim. But I found I couldn't answer her—I didn't know.

We shared clothes still damp from another girl's sweat. Once Susan said, "Wait," and she walked to me and kissed me twice, high on each cheekbone. Her lips were soft and moist and left faint lipstick marks on my face, which she stroked lightly with her fingers, one and then the other, into roses.

We began to relax, to take pictures we knew we would never show—silly shots of funny faces and Hercules poses. We laughed and laughed until our bellies ached, until tears streaked our faces, there in the small quiet house under the paintings of Hawaiian women who lay full and sleek with contentment. It could have been the champagne or the music, and it could have been the air, humid and warm as breath, so heavy it seemed to have its own weight—it was something to move through, and we moved through it the way one might draw a hand through a shallow bath. The green geckos shimmied over the walls, stopping from time to time to cock their arrow heads and *cluckcluckcluck* at us.

Over the afternoon we grew tired, and we moved more slowly, resting often, and we told one another things we'd never told anyone. The shadows, grown longer, waved and dipped in the wind over the walls, but the heat remained, held by those rooms, and we made no move to dress. Our hair heavy and limp, we wiped the makeup from our faces, and then it was just us, warm, flushed, and almost naked, like children. Something had changed: and it wasn't something to see or point to, it was something to feel, like a shift in the wind or the slight cool of deeper water. Imagine us there, unafraid, uncovered, for once.

There was a silence in which we considered ourselves. We took this in our hands, and we waited, not knowing what to do, whether to hold it, whether to give it away.

17

Show Me

K eith lived up the road, and I caught glimpses of him almost every day; but it was at Kanaha Beach, where he sometimes surfed, that I could look at him most openly. When he wasn't there, I watched the windsurfers who flitted like butterflies over the ocean, back and forth and back and forth, as if searching for something lost in the water below.

Keith didn't windsurf; he was a regular surfer, and a decent one. He preferred to long-board, like my brother Ken, who had taught me the summer before in Waikiki. Ever since then, since I had learned to paddle out and catch a wave—even though I was clumsy and the only waves I caught were small—I had felt closer to the boys of Hawaii. I could talk about wave height and fins, and I knew what a surfboard felt like under the body: stiffly buoyant and waxy-wet. I knew the twisty sensation in your gut and how riding a wave could make you feel like a god, if just for a moment.

When Keith and his friends came in from the waves, they'd shower off their boards and then themselves, arching under the spray, turning slow circles, lifting one arm and then the next, thrusting a hand in their shorts to let the water through. I'd watch them through the *kiawe* trees, where I lay facedown on my towel on the sand, head on folded arms. They never seemed shy, as I did when I used the outdoor shower, with people standing around waiting their turn and watching me.

Then they'd go to someone's car in the parking lot and get stoned one at a time, sitting face-out in the passenger seat, the door wide open. This allowed the person to watch the waves and talk, while giving him a little privacy; the cops circled the park every hour or so. The others would stand nearby, making me think of stalks of sugarcane, tall and slim and bandy. All of them naked except for swim trunks. Those trunks hung low and close on their hips, the bones there curved and poking through like the ends of a hanger through a coat. Keith was the slimmest, the shadowy *V* of his pelvis cupped inward.

That summer I would discover I could slip a finger in between the fabric and his skin and feel nothing but the heat of his body.

Viewed from a certain angle, the island of Maui is shaped like a woman. Trace its shape on a map and your finger will wind around curves. I was staying on the island for a few weeks with Ken's mother, Kaui. She lived in a small cottage on one end of the hourglass figure, on a protea-flower farm halfway up the slope of a dormant volcano, Haleakala. The other end of the island, marked by the Iao Mountains, was nearly always covered with clouds. From her back lanai I could see across Maui's narrow, flat waist—this stretch is the valley, a patchwork of sugarcane and pineapple fields, cut by a few two-lane highways. It is only seven miles across, a narrow band of green bordered by blue. In the morning, I had seen Keith surveying the beaches from his front step, looking for the white water that would signal a good swell.

Keith was older, in his mid-twenties. I liked his nonchalance, the way he'd casually slide his beer behind his back when a cop drove by. The way he sat on his lanai and propped his legs on the railing, smoking a cigarette and talking on the phone. He had a tattoo running the length of his calf, tribal-style, something Polynesian. He was haole, though: white. I knew he wasn't a nice guy, that he had dropped out in the eleventh grade from Maui High, that he made money selling the pot he grew under his house. He didn't drive because his license was suspended.

He wasn't anything, in fact, like my boyfriend, Jim, from school. Jim had come to the University of Hawaii for a year on exchange from Oregon. He wore khaki shorts and got drunk on three beers. His idea of rebellion was skiing in jeans. Although he was kind and smart, he was insecure. He complained that he couldn't study if he thought of me on the beach in my yellow bikini. "It's an invitation," he'd say. "Can you say *rape*?" And I'd reply: "Right. Right in the middle of Waikiki Beach. Right in front of ten thousand people."

That May, for my twenty-first birthday, he and I had taken a trip to New York. We'd stayed with his grandmother, a retired professor, in her elegant but musty apartment near Central Park. Jim had still been underage, so I bought us a bottle of rum and we ate pizza and then walked the streets of New York. As it grew late, the atmosphere changed, regular people were replaced by others more exotic and menacing, and Jim wanted to go back. We argued. I could tell he was scared, that he didn't feel the excitement I did, and I was intensely disappointed as we entered his grandmother's dark apartment, as if I'd failed a test or backed down from a challenge.

I knew Keith used to go out with a flower girl from Paia. I'd seen her one night, when I was at dinner with my father at the Makawao Steak House. She had come in, wound through the tables in a short sundress and high heels, the basket of leis and flowers tucked in the crook of her arm. She smelled like a perfume shop or a candy store, a place where too many things compete for attention. Nobody around us wanted any flowers, and when she walked by our table, I felt the same mix of guilt and annoyance I always did when these girls made their rounds and flashed their hopeful faces. She had the kind of job that seems glamorous until you see it up close: the smile stretched and stiff, freshly coated with lipstick. The rest of the makeup faded, the flesh of her feet straining at the bars of her sandals, the ten-year-old Honda at the curb, banged up and rusty.

I asked about her on the beach. Someone said they'd broken up because Keith had hit her, given her a fat lip. Still, I envied her—she was older, experienced. She would know what to do with Keith. He wouldn't have to show her—he wouldn't even have to ask. I had lavish fantasies about him, about how he'd dry me off as I stood dripping from the shower, massage lotion into me. And yet it was not tenderness I associated with him but something hard and unbending. I wanted to see him bend to me.

One afternoon he showed up at the door while Kaui was at work. I'd been reading. I was surprised to see him, but only a little. It was as if I knew we would meet, and the suspense had involved only where and when. He introduced himself, speaking in the slight pidgin accent of the haole kids who grow up in Hawaii and adopt the local style of speech. His eyes were almost gold, with green flecks, and they looked sore, as if he'd just been swimming or was stoned.

"I want to show you something," he said. Then he turned around and walked away, so I knew I was supposed to follow him.

"I've seen you around," he said as we walked up the red dirt road toward his place. This made me anxious and happy at once. He had tobacco in his teeth, small brown clumps. He smelled unclean but not unpleasant, as if he'd bathed in the ocean. I followed him to his small cabin and around to the shed behind it. I didn't know what to expect, but I figured at any moment he would try to kiss me, and I prepared myself. Instead of reaching for me, though, he turned to a case on a shelf and lifted out a rifle.

He held it flat on his palms, an offering. It looked worn, as if it had done a lot of shooting. The sun from the open door settled on us in a cone, and in the light and heat, the gun shone and sweated an odor of oil and metal. I thought of men who worked on cars, of how they smelled of greasy metal and sweat. To me, guns and cars and machines were associated with men. I believed knowledge about these things gave one a certain kind of power.

"Here," he said. I needed two hands to hold it. Before that day, I had never thought about shooting a gun. Guiding my arms from behind, he showed me how to aim. For a moment, I felt secure— lodged between the solid length of him and the gun tight in my hands. Then I became aware of the pressure of his body, the humid air that I could have grabbed and spread on my skin. I had an urge to pull the trigger, anything to cut the tension. He dropped his hands, then, and it ended. "Do you want to shoot it?" he asked. I said I did.

We walked up the road until we were far from any houses, until we couldn't see flowers anymore. It was hot, and the ashy dust settled over my shoes. Far below us, the harvested sugarcane fields were burning. Even from that distance, I could see the stalks of flame, so orange against the deep gray smoke. The smell came to us bitter and sweet, like a burned cake. Keith carried the gun on his back, secured by a strap. He was silent, with sweat tracking the sides of his brown face, and if it hadn't been for his surf trunks and Local Motion T-shirt, he could have been a gunslinger from a western film.

He stopped and pointed to a large cactus about twenty-five feet away. It had round, flat leaves like outstretched hands, with tiny clusters of white spikes sprouting from the tops. Nestling the butt of the gun into my shoulder, I bent my knees slightly, placed my feet shoulder-width apart, as Keith had told me to. I looked through the sight, and for a minute, I almost mistook the cactuses for human silhouettes, actors placed randomly on a slope. I tried to aim, but the gun wavered; I couldn't keep it steady. I felt Keith's fast breath, smelling sharp like sour cinnamon. His presence at once unnerved and reassured me.

I knew this excited him—that I excited him. I could see us there, held together by the act we were about to commit.

"Breathe out," he told me. "It'll relax you." That worked long enough for me to pull the trigger. The gun fired with a deafening clap and kicked back against me, leaving a bruise that would flower and spread for days. But all I knew was time had collapsed, so that a succession of events strangely compressed into the span of a trigger pull: the cactus bursting in a vicious blast of pulp, Keith howling wildly, the sting of gunpowder and sugarcane ash in my throat, the shadow of clouds rolling over us, and the quick cooling of the air.

Then I felt the silence that exists only in the aftermath of explosion. It didn't end until I touched the remains of the cactus and heard the slow drip of thin sap on the rocks.

That night I lay in bed and remembered the feel of his body behind me, his outline bigger than mine, the way I could fit into the safety of his body as if it were a cape. I wondered how he'd known I would want to shoot the gun. Could he see into me? Did he know the things I didn't even know yet that I wanted? He had said, "I knew you'd like it." And he was right. I had liked it, had liked knowing what it felt like to destroy something simply because I could.

For a while, we'd been the same. We had both been powerful, which was new for me. In my experience, power had always been something that was tossed back and forth between men and women, but it was the man who held it most of the time. Keith had let me briefly into his world, on his terms: he wanted to guide me, but there would be a price for my trespass. I knew this, so I was a little afraid of him, and of the things he might show me.

The next night Keith called and invited me over. As I walked up the road, I thought of Jim, of his eager kisses, his pride in his 3.8 GPA. Someone like Keith would intimidate and repel him. My father would be disappointed in me, would shake his head. He had different standards for me. My mother, though, would understand. She knew about the lure of a dangerous man.

Keith let me in and gave me a can of Budweiser. I thought of how Jim would have opened it for me first. We talked about shooting, about the boar he had killed on the island of Molokai. I showed him my bruise from the gun's kickback.

"You were good," he said. "You were hot." He said this approvingly but without enthusiasm.

A fan rotated back and forth, thoroughly surveying the small room. Newspapers and candy wrappers rose and fluttered in its path. The heat made me think of Keith's excitement when I'd aimed at the cactus, his fast breath: how my strong body, the gun in my hands, turned him on. Had he thought about it, too, the power he let me feel?

I realized I was ready to give, or accept, anything.

He reached and pulled me to him: this was what it would be, then. Of course. We knelt on his futon mattress, and holding me in his gaze the whole time, he pushed off the surf magazines and a pile of clothes. I let him undress me, down to my bathing suit, which I hadn't taken off from the beach that day; he just pushed the bra aside, and the crotch of my bikini, as if he couldn't wait; and he had sex with me right there, with the same intensity as when he surfed, or when he loaded the gun, as if all his pleasures were serious ones, and then for as long as it took a wave to break or a trigger's pull to kill something, he shot himself into me.

18

How to Get Home on Maui

I come in and Dad's at the bar. I know by the way he says the bartender's name, wet and slow to start, that he's had at least three rum and Cokes and no lunch.

"Shannon," he says, "here's my bouncing baby girl"—his standard greeting for me, though I'm twenty-four. I'm glad Shannon is on tonight, she's one of my favorites. Last year she had cancer, now she wears a wig. It sits tightly on her head as if she wants to make sure nothing short of a full gust could lift it off. She faces the people who sit at her bar, from the hopeful to the degraded, with the same tolerant good humor. This includes me and my father. She and the other staff are always glad to see me. *This man has a family, see how nice they are.* As if my presence cancels out all the days of drinking. But probably none of them really cares what's drawn him to drink. He tells me a story that happened at court, where he'd gone to pick up documents for Suzi, my stepmother. It's hilarious, and Shannon falls behind on her drink orders while she listens.

Of all his talents, he's best at storytelling, which he learned while growing up here in the islands. Here they call it "talk story," a way of conversing when no one believes anything and everyone believes everything. It's an art. My father says it's one of the main reasons people live in Hawaii. In fact, his novel, *Gone to Maui,* is full of talking story. Whenever I can, I like to remind whoever will listen that my dad's an author.

It's only me and Dad at the bar, a mediocre place in Kahului that tends more to locals than tourists, which is why we like it. He and his pals come in for lunch on Tuesdays. The owners made up little brass plates with their names engraved and stuck them right on the table, like they're members of the board or some important club. Sometimes I join them, and my dad will hand over a menu and tell me to get the French dip or the mahimahi—whatever he wants a bite of. He's not a big eater. The booze fills him up, and that's why he's so thin. In his younger days he was a skillful bodysurfer, knowing just when to catch the wave before it broke, and when I was a little girl, I used to watch him all day, cheering from the shore.

The place is dim, lit only by neon beer signs and the light along the bar—the kind of light that can show the wear and tear on the face. In here my dad looks sixty, but he's just over fifty. Still, even dive bars feel sort of nice in Hawaii. You get fresh flowers in your drinks, and just outside is a sweet tropical breeze. In the background they're playing the Pahinui Brothers—the happy Hawaiian music that always makes me think of my hula lessons in high school. The smoke from Shannon's cigarette floats around her and it's almost sexy, how it curls in on itself slow and smooth. She looks at me and my dad like it's all very clear to her, like she has us and everything else figured out.

I order a mango daiquiri, and my dad shakes his head slowly, as if he's disappointed in my taste. He slurps his rum and Coke.

"Have some pretzels," I tell him, and pass the wooden bowl. He needs to eat. Later, we go outside and find out the keys are locked in his car. Shannon calls us a cab.

We wait for our ride outside, where we have a first-class view of the Bank of Hawaii parking lot. The sun's setting somewhere, Lahaina-side. Over the door, a speaker pipes the music from inside, an old favorite of mine from Cecilio and Kapono. I snap off a pink blossom from a nearby plumeria tree and tuck it behind my ear. The perfume from the tree is so thick it could've been sprayed on.

"You come, too, okay?" he says when the song ends. "Come eat with us. She's making that artichoke thing, the one with the mayonnaise."

Okay. I tell him sure. I'm beat from an afternoon of writing press releases and making phone calls that aren't returned. The daiquiris swim in my stomach, and I feel a little nostalgic. When I was at the University of Hawaii studying journalism, I used to visit my dad all the time at the Manoa Chart House, his favorite hangout. He knew everyone's name, even the busboys and flower girls. I used to watch him—the way he'd get a read on the place, then say something funny or interesting at just the right time, and before I knew it he would have made friends with everyone there. He liked to make people feel good; he did it by making you laugh, or by asking questions that made you feel smart in answering.

For these reasons I loved his company. Sometimes I'd bring my friend Richelle to the Chart House with me, and Dad would show us off. We'd always create a little stir. We were eighteen or nineteen and we looked good. *Two* bouncing baby girls. We felt safe with Dad because people respected him as a family man, even though he didn't really have a job that they knew of. The bartender would give us drinks without question, and then Dad would spring for some sashimi or oyster shots and we'd tell him the best gossip about the UH athletes.

We loved getting high on piña coladas, priming ourselves for the evening's event, usually a campus party. My dad told us jokes and teased us in a way that filled us with confidence, telling us we'd better go easy on Honolulu—the city couldn't handle the likes of us. Often we stayed a lot longer than we'd planned. The tradition was to give a toast to my dad before we left, and I was always really proud at that moment and full of love for the way he treated us with respect, like we were adults.

That was a few years back, when life seemed a lot more open, with bigger options and more of them. I thought I was going to be the next Diane Sawyer. I actually thought it was possible.

. . .

People are walking by us into the bar . . . two Japanese women in short skirts, a young Filipino man with a cigarette, a haole man. All locals, going to dinner, most likely. Dad and I step aside into the light to let them pass. No one looks at us directly; instead they throw glances like fishing lines that reel in the picture of us: an almost old man and a young woman, both unsteady and with eyes too red. After a time a glowing moon eases up over Iao Valley, and the patterns on the surface make it look like a dusty bulb hung up in the sky.

"Well-would-you-look-at-that," my dad says very slowly, as if the sight is so amazing it's affected his power of speech.

The cab pulls up, and Dad and I fumble our way in back. The driver just sits there and doesn't open the door. He's white, and I feel the same little shock I always do when I see a haole working in a blue-collar job. It's kind of a rare occurrence in the islands, since whites are a minority here, and to me we always seem out of place.

The car smells faintly of wet carpet and something artificial and lemony. And cigarettes. I stick my fingers in the rips in the seat. My dad looks at me but can't quite focus. The driver is a beefy guy in his late thirties, and it's an effort for him to turn around in his seat, but he twists partway and checks out my dad. His brow furrows as if my dad's a puzzle he's going to figure out. The guy's unshaven, with big eyes and long cow lashes, the kind women usually go nuts over. The kind of guy you think could be real attractive if he'd just take better care of himself.

"You got a destination?"

"Kula," I tell the driver, who pivots his gaze to me then. His pupils are scary-dilated in the interior light of the cab. He turns forward and gets out a cigarette and asks for the address. I figure he should ask if we mind the smoking, and that he doesn't seems significant in a bad way.

"It's on Kimo Drive," my dad tells him.

I add, "It's below Kula Lodge." I've been to the house only a couple of times, and there aren't any streetlights up there. It's a long drive, and I'm hoping my dad won't fall asleep; he looks so tired. I try not to look at the driver, but the rearview mirror holds a perfect rectangle of his eyes. It pulls me like a TV screen in a bar.

"You got cash?"

"Oh yeah," my dad says, nodding gravely with lips pursed, and he gets out his own cigarette. One thing about my dad, no matter how many drinks he's had, he still lights up as cool as James Dean. We drive down Haleakala Highway, and I think about the way Ken and I sat in the back of my dad's cab in San Francisco, almost fifteen years ago. It's a weird thought, and I put it out of my mind. My dad tells the driver, who has informed us his name's Darrell, all the jokes he'd told Shannon and then me at the bar. I laugh again because they're funny and so is my dad, the way he cracks himself up sometimes—he's laughing into the cup of his hand like it's a walkie-talkie. The driver nods after each joke and points his finger up in the air. "Good one," he says, after the last one, and then, "I got a funny story.

"I was hitchhiking with my buddy Chuck about three years back, outside of Reno. We were gonna visit his ex-wife in Carson City. You know Nevada?"

"I've been to Reno," I say softly. This guy's only pretending to be comfortable. He's too wired; his fingers grip the headrest. You have to be careful when a man like this gets behind the wheel.

"So we've been walking and it's hot. Not like island heat, this is dry heat, oven heat. Bakes you like a batch of cookies."

My dad grunts.

"So this guy picks us up and tells us he's goin' to *Mus*tang Ranch—you know, the whorehouse." Darrell draws out "Mustang Ranch" like it's the name of something good to eat. He pauses to get our reaction in the mirror.

"My dad wrote a book once," I say. I don't want to hear his whorehouse story.

"That so. Stories, I could tell you stories. You could write a book about the stories I know. Chuck himself was shot right in front of me one time in Denver. But he survived—you bet. Hard as nails, man, that guy was *hard as nails.*"

Darrell pulls out a shiny flask and sips and doesn't offer us any. I notice my dad notice.

A sign for Kula swims up in the lights as we pass: eight miles, I think it said.

Must be some kind of game or rodeo in Makawao, because there's traffic going up-country. All the way up the mountain, cars' brake lights wind their way and vanish at the top like tiny pairs of red eyes peering over the edge. Darrell is tense, keeps talking about the girls at Mustang Ranch. Dad and I have become real quiet in back. I realize I'm drunk, that information is coming through a thick screen, fighting its way in. I settle on the simplest thing until I get it clear, then move on to the next. Like the back of this guy's head. I've memorized it, mostly because it's so close I could slap him if I wanted. Hair the color of watery rum, combed slick like a cat licked it in place. Even in the dark, his skin looks raw, tinged red with sunburn or some uncomfortable emotion. Ears close to the head and delicate. I think of him at Mustang Ranch. Those ears would be real sensitive—a woman with a notion could bring a guy like that to his knees. The swirl of his scalp is pale beneath the thinning hair of his crown, and the truth of this small weakness gives me a shot of strength.

"You like country?" Darrell asks as he pops in a tape of banjo music.

"No," I say.

My dad says okay, but just not the Nitty Gritty Dirt Band. That's his wife's favorite, she's from Texas, and she plays it too much. She's probably playing it right now as she waits for us up on this dark mountain.

We're passing through Pukalani, and the temperature dips as we climb. It's cooler by ten degrees, at least. Up farther in Kula, it's so chilly a lot of people use electric blankets when they sleep.

And Darrell's saying now, "I once picked up two girls and it turned out they didn't have any money when I dropped 'em off."

Please stop, I think, and I look at my dad, but he's staring down at his skinny legs. As he's gotten older he's gotten weaker, even frail. He hardly even plays golf anymore, and he never goes to the beach. It makes me feel protective, and I hate this driver with his muscles, his rude bulk. He turns right on 37 and we're past all the lights of Pukalani now. It's dark, but the moonlight's given the land a sepia sheen, like an old photograph. God, it's beautiful.

The driver keeps looking at me in the rearview mirror, I can feel it. His eyes are big and dark, and I wonder if he's even watching the road. *Asshole,* I think. I'd like to ask him what he's looking at, but I don't want trouble, and what would I do if he started something? My father's not a fighter; he's the gentlest person I know. I've never seen him raise his hand to anyone or even mention a time that he had. He hates confrontation as I much as I do. Still, you want to know that when it comes down to it, your father will save you—he'll be there.

Then Upper Kimo Drive presents itself, and I tell the guy to *slow down*—he's taking the curves too fast and the road's damp, we've got mist all around. But it's like he doesn't hear me. I know it's about a mile up this road, somewhere, but will we recognize it? In the dark, it all looks the same. But then I see the fence.

"Okay, it's up here, just after the white fence there on your left," I tell him, but he just goes right by.

I look over at my father, who seems resigned. I sense that even though he's drunk, he knows I'm uncomfortable, that I'll be in a lot of uncomfortable situations, that he can never do anything to prevent them. Maybe this lifetime of drinking has stolen more than his strength—maybe it's taken his faith. He doesn't believe he can save himself, let alone me.

"Hey," my dad says. "I think you missed the, the—"

Darrell pulls the car onto the dirt shoulder about twenty yards past our driveway. He shuts off the engine and the headlights with it. Doesn't say anything, just stares into the sudden dark before him, the mist that swirls like dust. A nearby porch light reveals the three of us, this strange triangle. Somewhere a dog barks to no answer. My dad pulls out his wallet and digs out two twenties, and then we help each other out of the car.

We never talked of Darrell to my dad's wife. I'm not even sure my dad remembered it in the morning. The truth is, I was more worried about protecting my father's dignity than myself. This has always been my job, self-appointed and pointless. But the irony is that in the end, it's myself I'm trying to save. We're tied together, my father and I. If he falls, I'm going down, too.

I live in the Midwest now, and my father's still on Maui, now divorced. He's dying, and he lies in my brother's back bedroom, the final stages of liver failure leaving him cold and sleep-laden. Now and then I go to a bar called George's. It's nothing like the bars I used to go to in Hawaii. They don't put flowers or umbrellas in your drinks, and if you want a fresh daiquiri or a good mai tai, forget it. But the beer tastes the same and the cigarettes smell the same and after a while the bartender even sounds familiar.

One night I was standing next to a guy whose loneliness was so old and so big I had to push it aside to sit down. In the light of the Coors sign, his ruined face took on tragic proportions. He bought me a drink and then said, "Why don't you make a toast. To whatever you want." I thought for just a moment, and then we raised our glasses high and drank to my father.

19

The Dive Bar Tours

I wake up in December and I'm twenty-six and married and living in Spokane, a city that spreads over the dry prairies of eastern Washington like a slow burn. Maui floats on turquoise waters on the other side of the world. I left the island last summer to get married and pursue a master's degree because I thought I knew what I was doing, because I was tired of the heat, of my PR job, and because of my suspicion that I was going nowhere with my life. I believed it was time to get serious, which is hard to do on a tropical island.

Spokane is my husband's home; I have no other connection to it. I'd prefer a place like Seattle or Portland or Boulder. If cities were ice-cream flavors, Spokane would be vanilla. Not French or vanilla bean, just plain. Our condominium overlooks downtown, perched on a hill in a row of other condos like a bunch of crows on a wire. Neighbors surround us on four sides, eating and sleeping and bathing—I doubt much fucking goes on, since I haven't seen anyone under sixty—but I try not to think about it. Despite the view, the feeling in the place is one of *insulation*.

My graduate school homework adds to this muffledness: I'm buried under mountains of inscrutable reading assignments that give me regular night sweats. Every day I cart my ignorance into the classroom. I also have a sickening feeling that my marriage isn't going to work, that it's all a mistake. The winter, thick and severe, gathers and hurls itself at me on a daily basis. Regret has become something I breathe.

I'd planned to get a practical degree in technical writing, but the classes are so dry I've taken a fiction workshop, taught by a short, testy woman who's just published a novel I can't get through. She inspires me nonetheless, and I'm seriously thinking of ditching the technical writing for creative. It was in the fiction class that I first heard about the Dive Bar Tours. These excursions are part entertainment and part research, and everyone is hush-hush about them. They'd been organized in the fall by some of the graduate writers. I wasn't part of their crowd—they were mainly single, ironic, artsy young men—but I'd shown I could write a decent story. One day they invited me along, and it felt like a great honor. I find myself willing to belong to anything other than the life I've chosen.

A year ago, my husband, Paul, proposed to me and I said yes. He decided to leave his easy-street job as a condo manager on Maui and buy a printing franchise that promised us riches. He didn't know anything about manufacturing, or wholesale business, but he'd felt the same need to get serious back here on the mainland. We traveled all the way to the corporate headquarters in Florida to check out the franchise and make sure it was on the up-and-up. The office was impressive and we were taken nightly to fabulous seafood restaurants. We'd be investing a lot of money, but this was a sure thing, all signs pointed to go.

The business has lost money from the start. My husband's savings account bleeds like a body full of bullets while he and I watch in bewildered dismay. This franchise had cleaned up all over the country, and ours should have, too, because we've followed the same business plan. Franchises are like a giant connect-the-dots game; success depends on replication of the original idea. Instead of a large metropolis for our customer base, we have a giant rural region: eastern Washington, northern Idaho, and all of Montana. It's like the frontier all over again. My husband spends weeks traveling to print shops in towns so tiny they show up only on certain maps. These road trips make for a hard and lonely existence, and the toll shows in his drawn face; he appears dazed by the turn his life has taken. I picture him grinding along two-lane highways, traversing prairies and mountain passes, his Pathfinder stuffed with promotional material and fast-food containers and his own anxious ambition. In the process he becomes a stranger to me—and because I can forget, and feel free again, I begin to enjoy his absences.

The tours take place in downtown Spokane, which is an eerie place, especially on a winter night. The streets are strangely deserted, partly because of the skywalks, those futuristic glass tunnels that connect the second floors of many of the buildings and keep shoppers away from the ground, weather, and unfortunate people. Maps direct you from point A to point B: you can crisscross the city in these tubes for hours and never breathe anything but seventy-two-degree air. All this achieves is a sense of lonely separateness, and I avoid the skywalks accordingly.

To get to the dive bars you have to connect with the street. There is no other way in.

The tour: at nine P.M., about once a month, half a dozen people meet at the downtown campus and then, for the rest of the night, traipse from bar to bar—establishments with names like the T&A Lounge, the 2 A.M. Club, Vic's Place, the Water Trough. After exactly one drink, we head to the next place, traveling close to buildings through whirling snow, like a wintry pack of thieves. We never run out of spots. Spokane is home to a lot of dive bars; they huddle in pockets of buildings and hide in folds of forgotten neighborhoods. But there is a kind of pattern—you can drift from one windowless bar to the next as if following a scent on the wind. I bet if you looked at a map of Spokane's dive bars from above, they'd form a constellation.

I've married a man fourteen years older. We threw a big bash of a wedding last summer at a grand hotel on the Columbia River. People had a good time, but to me the whole event felt like a staged show. But that's how weddings are—you even rehearse them, for God's sake. The worst part for me was my dress, which began to symbolize the forced nature of the whole arrangement. Despite the energy I put into finding the right one, it was a disaster. I had a seamstress make the first dress for me using my own design, thinking I could be thrifty. Traditional, off-the-shoulder, made of thick satin, it looked absurd on me, hanging like a large, collarless bathrobe. With three weeks to go, I had another made but picked the wrong fabric. The linen blend bunched along the seams. It looked like I had made it myself while watching TV. I'll never forget my stepmother's reaction when she saw me twenty minutes before the ceremony. In the span of two seconds her face registered shock, dismay, and then a determined resignation: it was much too late to do anything. She took a quick inhale and said, "It's fine." My hair, though, looked great.

The groom and I hardly talked that night. I felt distant, scared, aware that the next morning and its solemn finality would come all too soon, and this put me in a desperate mood. I hung out with the band behind the hotel during their breaks. We drank beer, and I flirted with the singer. I'd have run off with him if only he'd asked.

Paul had a lot of friends at the wedding; most of them live in Spokane. He's known them since college and before, and they're all well off and settled into their lives, into careers and children and investments. One wife is my age, but her four-year-old son hangs continually from her limbs like a sling. We gather for the occasional cocktail party and football game, and subtle tensions and flirtations bubble under the surface like trapped air. Everyone has a lake house or a ski cabin whose acquisition and upkeep provide a steady stream of conversation.

At these events, my attempts at playing the gracious, witty wife take on surreal proportions. I find myself watching TV commercials for behavior tips. The Spokane wives have perfected their routines over the years—gym, child care, shopping trips to Seattle. Kitchens are tailored to needs like a fine suit to a body. Laundry is done properly and without apparent effort; dishes match, and even pots and pans come in sets. Picnic baskets complete with coordinating napkins and silverware are tucked neatly in the closet. I've never met anyone like these women; my mother might as well have come from a foreign country. I keep waiting for someone to tell me what to do and how to do it.

The tours are scheduled randomly; someone makes a phone call. Everyone dresses down and dark, and we bring our egos, which are at once large and full of fear. There is the sense that we're bad actors and that eventually we'll be exposed. We sit around tables in rooms where smoke hovers in white clots. Old men are strung along the bar like sad ornaments on a branch.

We get drunker through the night but keep the rule of one drink per bar. The drinks we order will infuse us with the tragic nostalgia that crawls up the walls and lurks in the corners. We discuss Kerouac, Burroughs, Bukowski. I always get one of my dad's drinks, a Gibson, which gives me a certain cachet with the guys, I suppose because it has a Gatsby mood to it. The drink comes with cocktail onions, like the toy in a Cracker Jack box.

Jonathan orders blended margaritas because he likes how the blender shakes up the place. He calls it his version of the drum roll. He's pudgy, with a soft, round face, and he wears black leather to compensate. Another of the fiction writers, Curtis, has a strange habit of swallowing bottle-cap-size clumps of toothpaste from a tube he keeps in his breast pocket. He says the gel variety is best.

"It's an outrageous rush," he tells me once, offering his tube of Aquafresh.

Each time we get together, we talk about the pilgrimage we'll make to Hemingway's grave in Ketchum, Idaho. We all laugh real hard like we're having fun. We stumble to the next bar.

"Look at those dumb fucks," someone says, pointing to an insanely bright floor of offices ten stories above us, where we can see a few people apparently still engaged in some sort of business. It's like looking through a TV screen into another planet. I wonder if any of Paul's friends are working up there.

When he isn't on the road, Paul stations himself at the office, a cavernous place he rented just on the edge of downtown. If you yell in there, the words echo back. Paul dropped a lot of money to remodel it with nice businesslike carpet and paint, but no amount of plants or pictures can blot out the emptiness that surrounds us. The whole project is a nightmare from which we wake for only a few minutes at a time.

No one works for us long; either we have to fire them or they leave, sensing that the business is doomed. Still, applications stream in, filled out by needy folks hoping to be a Customer-Service Person, Printer, Typesetter, or Delivery Person. Most of them we turn away. Some look like they've just crawled out of the Spokane River. Others are nice and hopeful but with the wrong experience or none at all. We feel haunted by some of them, sure our rejection has been the last straw and they've joined the other luckless under the bridge or out at the railroad yards.

Our current typesetter is very fat—his is not a stately but a sweaty, unnerving fat. He scoots along on his stool like a giant M&M on wheels. He is much too meticulous. I come upon him staring wide-eyed at the computer screen as he trims a logo magnified fifty times, pixel by pixel, erasing rough edges that no human eye could see at actual size. His glacial pace throws off both the camera and the printing sequence. We learn quickly that manufacturing is like a precarious game of dominoes; the smallest delay can provoke a disaster down the line.

Our customer-service person fooled us with her professional clothes and manner, but over time we realized she made mistakes that probably cost us in the thousands of dollars—we'll never know. After we confronted her, she maintained her innocence indignantly, slinging fierce, wounded glances as she efficiently packed her things in a box. She intrigued me, though, with her neat ways and her short orange hair.

I've begun to hate the place and its smell of failure, the stream of catastrophes so trivial but so defeating—a color slightly off, or a name misspelled or too big or too small, and if we do get a job right, it's often a day late or delivered to the wrong address. Many nights my husband works long past midnight, hunched over a light board, trying to center a quarter-inch photo of a hammer on a hardware store's letterhead. We make so many mistakes that at least half our work comes under the heading "redo." The problem is that no one really knows what's going on. Now and then a couple of guys swoop up from Florida and survey our operation, nodding with grave expressions.

The urge to get on a Greyhound bus overwhelms me. So does my guilt.

I do enjoy the marmots across the busy four-lane street that fronts the office. They live in a wall of boulders that runs along the street for half a block. In between whizzing cars, you can see small beige animals tumble in and out of the rocks. I watch them through the window from my desk. How do they survive in that small strip of stones? I feel close to them because they seem more out of place than I am.

For my husband's forty-second birthday, I plan a big surprise party in Coeur d'Alene, a resort area just over the Idaho border. All his friends book rooms at the main hotel, and Paul and I are supposed to meet them at a wine and jazz bar. I hire a limo and glam myself up; I'm wrapped in tight black Lycra, and the limo driver drops his clipboard when he sees me. I have champagne and a tape I've made of sexy songs. Paul and I haven't touched each other in weeks; I'm sure this will do the trick.

We pick Paul up and he's exhausted as usual, though stupidly I've expected him to be different. The ride is a disappointment for both of us, a monumental setup. I try seducing him, and he tries to go along. I know he wants to for me. I realize too late that I've done what I wanted to do instead of what he might want or need. I'd like to call off the whole thing, but instead I just keep drinking champagne, and by the time we reach the restaurant, I can hardly walk straight. At the table all I see are familiar strangers. During dinner I listen to discussions with dangerous undercurrents, where thoughts swim like ugly fish, and comments dart and nip. I try to stay above water. An hour later Paul asks his brother to take me to our hotel room, where I dive into a deep and welcome oblivion.

Most of the dive bars are calm places, like eternal waiting rooms where strangers come in, drink for a while, then leave in the same random way. It's like some bizarre game of musical chairs, and I bet if you watched it on high-speed film, you'd eventually see the same people going through the same motions. It seems to me there must be some logic here.

Some of the bars have a family atmosphere, and entering one of these is like stepping into someone's living room by mistake. People look at you strangely. In one bar the ceiling stands as high as two men and a TV hangs way up in one corner. A handful of patrons gaze up in awe. I catch a glimpse of a cooking show. The Chinese chef is slicing lush mushrooms for coq au vin. Hot dogs rotate on a spit behind greasy glass on the bar and a laminated card advertises them for seventy-nine cents apiece.

Mostly these dive bars are subdued, because drinking here is a serious business. On the very first tour, one of the students jump-started the jukebox in the bar, but the sudden shot of sound was a frightening thing, full of expectation, as out of place as party hats and sparklers. We're out of place, too. Our presence is tolerated and ignored. To the great amusement of their customers, the bartenders (these places have no cocktail waitresses) make great productions of checking our IDs, even though most of us are clearly past twenty-one. Next to these old-timers, our youth is almost obscene. We ooze audacity—it's like we've strolled in stark naked. Patrons look up at us with bleary surprise, as if we've been churned up out of their hallucinations.

I walk home under quiet snow, grab a comforter and wrap it around me, then go out onto the deck, which is about the size of a double bed. I try to steady myself, since the deck is rolling under me. The city of Spokane fills the view, and I'm on the prow of a boat heading straight for it. Then I remember that this deck isn't moving, that the ocean is about eight hours west by car. The February air scrapes my tired throat. Snowflakes wander aimlessly, and though they all look the same, I know different. In a corner of my mind I'm aware of the presentation I have to do tomorrow, forty-five minutes on a nineteenth-century rhetorician named Richard Whately. I've been dreading it for weeks.

The city is going to sleep without me. I can hear its distant, set-tling hum, and now and then a bleating car horn, like the last forlorn hurrah of a New Year's Eve party. The city lights throb under the snow, and the image could be pretty, depending on your mood. I stick out my hand, blot it from my sight.

One day I'm sitting at home on the sectional couch that floats on the lake of orange carpet. I hate the way my toes disappear into the carpet's scratchy softness, so I prop my feet on the coffee table. Paul comes home, and it's the first time he's been back in seven days. Everything about him is rumpled, even his face and hands. He looks like he's folding into himself. I try to picture him coming in from sailing at Kanaha Beach, hauling his windsurfer through the waves and onto the white sand. Then I remember—that man isn't here anymore.

I tell him I'm very unhappy.

"Is it school?" This has been my excuse for months, and it always satisfies him.

"No," I say. "It's us. It's me. I don't think I can keep doing this."

He looks at me like he can't believe the destruction of his life extends this far, has entered even his home. And then the surprise fades because he's known all along and hasn't wanted to face it, either.

The confession makes me tired—I could fall asleep while talking to him, I'm so tired. I know I've handed him what he will see as more evidence of his own failure, but I can't hide it anymore. We stare at each other from across an ocean.

I make an appointment with a marriage counselor, and Paul gamely agrees, though it's clear he's wary. The counselor is short and chunky, and his wedding band gleams with a self-satisfied reproach. He doesn't look like the sympathetic type. Paul answers most of his questions with jokes to ease the tension, but the counselor always waits a beat before smiling, as if letting us know he's being indulgent. He's about my husband's age, and my professors' age, and I fight the image of myself as an errant schoolgirl sent to the principal's office.

We tell him about our fun-filled courtship, the inter-island trips and bike rides through the pineapple fields of West Maui, morning tennis, the long walks on Ka'anapali Beach during which we planned our wedding.

"Relationships are like reservoirs," the counselor says. "You keep adding to the reservoir over time as you overcome obstacles, and then when things get tough, you draw from it."

He looks at us and holds up his thumb and index finger, with the space of about a grape between them. "This is how big your reservoir was when you got married."

We both stare and nod at the pitiful state of our reservoir, which apparently ran dry somewhere between the move from Hawaii to the mainland and the wedding, the opening of a doomed business, and my humbling career switch from public-relations account executive to student.

"Do you see? You had no time to build up your reservoir," he says, in a tone that suggests it's too late to begin now.

At Vic's Place, I study the few women I see. One woman has tremendous black eyebrows, like smears of tar, like a child drew wings over her eyes with a Magic Marker. I wish I were that brave—to let one piece of my body stand for everything else. Some of the bar guys check me out, offer themselves to me with their sad eyes, their hope propped up like an old fence. Others aren't so defeated, and they eye me squarely, as if the decision were theirs and not mine. One swarthy-looking man stretches, revealing his band of a belly and the word VIRGIN tattooed across it. I think, *When were you ever a virgin?*

I have a slight crush on one of my classmates, a poet from Chicago with small rimless glasses and a great head of hair. I send him sexy looks and nod at his Orwell references, but he's searching for something much more drastic than I can provide. I feel saddened by this inadequacy, a feeling that compresses inside me over the night.

The good times keep you going, and then the memories of good times carry you a little farther. Early in the fall, when it was still warm, Paul and I would take our bikes to his family's lake cabin. We rode around the lake, the fresh air and exercise a temporary rejuvenation. Later, while he puttered around on the shore, I'd lie on the dock, feeling it sway under the length of me, listening to the slap of waves under the wood.

In the evening, we always took the boat out. We'd circle the lake looking at the other cabins, some empty, some with families still on their docks and small strips of beach. Paul knew all their histories, who owned what and such, because he'd been coming to the lake forever, since he was a kid. Hearing his stories and seeing these gathered families always left me melancholy—it was the normalcy I'd wanted as a child. For as long as I can remember, I've envied the people for whom the summer cabin sat in the middle of their life like a table centerpiece. But it's too late for me now. It's not, anymore, that I don't know how—it's that I don't even want it. And I'm sorry, because I thought I could do this, and do this with Paul; it was what he wanted, and I led him to believe I wanted it, too.

I remember how our boat glided through deep green water on which I could see my reflection but nothing beyond. The tinny melodies from distant radios would drift over the water toward us, like signals we couldn't decipher. Each cabin presented its own portrait of how to live, and we pointed out the ones we liked best, imagining ourselves there. Our voices and manner were quiet, the way people are when they see something beautiful, and out of reach.

At midnight we find a table at the Sunset and cling to it.

The trouble is, we don't have the guts to ask these men about their lives, so we make up their histories.

"That guy?" Calvin tips his glass in the direction of a heavy man who nuzzles his drink as if he likes the way it smells. "That guy, he might have been a local prizefighter."

Most of the guys in our group are just slumming. They are purely voyeurs; this both shames and consoles them—they know they'll never end up here, and the relief makes them uncomfortable. But a few of us know the fine line that separates our lives from ones in which these bars could become a regular retreat.

I feel a kind of affinity with the men from the dive bars, and sympathy. Too many wear no socks, and outside, the windchill is about fifteen. One guy has cheeks so red with drink I can see them from the other side of the room. He looks like a clown who's given up. Another guy was handsome a hundred years ago, but now the capillaries in his skin have assembled into maps, and if you follow one of those trails, you'll end up somewhere in Utah or the Dakotas or one of your bad dreams.

We say we're on these tours to find material for our writing, to find characters, but what we're searching for is the real thing, hoping we can find it here where all the bullshit has been stripped away. We want answers, though the truth is, we're looking for something that can't be found anywhere, that no one can explain, not our lovers or parents or teachers. But the people in these bars, these men and women, they have stories swung around their necks. Epic tragedies hover over them like personal clouds, and we think if anyone knows what's important, if anyone knows what mistakes to avoid, they do.

Midevening, I'm standing outside the baggage claim at Spokane's airport, waiting for Paul to pick me up. I've come back from Easter weekend with my mother and new stepfather, Steve. My mother is sympathetic and quietly supports my choice to leave Paul. "I'm not surprised," she said, though she had a hard time explaining why. She thinks that although he has a good heart, he's reserved, even inhibited. "It's just a feeling," she said. I think she simply knows when something's over and it's time to move on. For the first time I'm grateful for her past, for all my fathers. She can't argue with my decision to leave Paul—she has no right, and we both know it.

Paul's late. It's cold and the airport is nearly empty; most of the passengers have been picked up or gotten their cars. I feel a small seed of hope begin to grow: *Maybe he won't show up.* I consider this the way one might a brilliant but dangerous idea. Cars roll off the exit toward the airport, and each time it's something else—a pickup or large car—I feel a shiver of relief. With each minute passing the hope grows. *Please don't let him show up,* I whisper to no one. At this point I don't care what's happened to him: maybe he ran off finally;

maybe he's met another woman. Or—I tiptoe with horror around this—maybe an accident. Something painless, quick. I taste guilt like acid in my mouth, in my gut. I watch the road, which remains, for now, empty.

I don't tell Paul about the tours. We haven't talked much since we quit the counseling; when we talk, it's about the business. He wouldn't approve, that's a given. Why would he? His wife spending the evening with a bunch of guys, getting drunk at the seediest places in town. I amuse myself by imagining what his friends' wives would say. The topic doesn't come up anyway, because I go when he's out of town. In the meantime we drift from each other like rafts on a sea, slow and inevitable. We're both letting this go, and I couldn't touch him even if I wanted to.

But if he did ask, I'd tell him that maybe a dive bar is the farthest from the marriage I can get. Or the closest to my father. He's always with me in these places—he's there, in fact, wherever the booze is. This is my father's territory. Watching these men, maybe I'll understand what compels him to drink. What has happened to these men that they've ended up here? I believe everyone thrives on a certain amount of pain: it's a fuel that can motivate us to act, to strive, to run from one lover to the next—to do whatever we must do. The pain is replenished along life's difficult road, and it keeps storing up until someday it hurts too much. Paul and his successful friends keep earning and struggling, putting on a false front. The men in these bars, though, are more honest. They drink openly to numb the pain. Like my father, they are closer to it.

My life feels as if it's been cleaved into two parts, and I'm a stranger in both, an impostor no matter where I find myself. What I learn at school is precisely that I don't know much of anything, and all the theory thrown at me is another language I have to learn. It slips obscurely through my mind like sand through fingers. Only in the bars do I see anything that seems real anymore, that's not hidden or whitewashed.

I have questions. Am I a young suburban wife of a business owner? An aspiring writer who needs to be alone? Or something else entirely? What I do know is that there is no hope of these worlds intersecting.

On these tours, we're filling ourselves with fluid and stories, like we're all just lonely, empty vessels. In the end, no matter why we're here, we drink until the dignity's gone and the truth finally presents itself to us. We're no different from these people. I'm no different from my father or my mother. There is no escape.

These places are everywhere, and the stories never cease and the people never leave. I worry about it. These are places I could end up—and who will save me if I do?

•

20

Release

Female Visitors
Items Not Allowed:
>Tank tops
>Halter tops
>Tops that bare the midriff
>Low-cut, sleeveless, or cutout shirts
>Shirts or dresses which expose undergarments, cleavage, or back
>Culottes, skirts, dresses shorter than one inch above the top of the kneecap
>Wraparound skirts, shirts, or dresses with full-length openings
>Dresses or skirts too tight to allow pat search of inner leg
>Clothing with holes
>Spandex, Lycra, or other rubberized or elasticized garments
>Garments made of sheer or transparent fabric

I ask myself on the drive west out of Spokane, the empty road cutting through wasted snow, snow pocked and gray after weeks of dry cold. I ask myself because others ask me. If I want to teach writing, why not intern at the high school, the nursing home? Why a prison? A men's prison, medium security. My students could be murderers or rapists, drug dealers, transferred for good behavior to this eastern Washington facility for the rest of their terms. But they still need help. My class, I tell myself, will provide an expressive outlet for these felons. They can tell me their stories and undergo catharsis, and when they get out, I will have helped them gather back the seed of their humanity. But if I'm quiet long enough, I'll consider the truth: I want to get close, close to whatever shadow it is that follows these men. The thought unnerves me, and I turn up the radio. In the distance the prison is lit up, a stadium for villains, and all around it is dark.

I'm hidden in a thick black tunic of a sweater; its turtleneck is too tight. Wool stockings confine my legs under a brown skirt. As advised, I wear flat shoes that I can run in. Over the weeks, I'll shed clothes the way some women shed inhibitions, carefully and one at a time. On the night of the fight, I'll be wearing just a T-shirt and black, narrow pants.

I look up, and Mike, who's here for drug running, is staring at me. "You're so intelligent," he says. He says it like he wants to say something else. Certain personal comments and questions are okay: *Are you a writer? You are a good teacher.* But others are off limits: *You're in good shape—do you work out?* His hair is glossy, caught in a long ponytail. He is not handsome, but there is something.

The volunteer coordinator warned us many times that the men are manipulative. *Do not bring them stamps or newspapers. Tell them nothing personal. They will use it against you.* Mike has a son with cerebral palsy whom he has not seen in three years, and one day he passes me a note: "Can you help me find my boy?"

Offender Manipulation
1. Be aware of the verbal and nonverbal messages you send, watch body language.
2. Know your personal and professional goals. Understand your value system.
3. Learn to be assertive and use the word "NO" appropriately.

4. Do not do anything you would be ashamed to share with your peers or supervisor.

The men in my class aren't supposed to ask if I'm married. That's a "boundary issue." But I know they wonder. I don't wear my ring. I am full of secrets they sense but cannot name. I could reveal them one at a time, if I wanted, in subtle ways. For instance: *This passage really captures the isolation one can feel in a marriage.*

The condo in Spokane is carpeted thickly, even the bathrooms, orange stuff crawling up the base of the walls like thick fur. I can walk around and make no sound. No one would know I'm here: I disappear in my home, which is not my home; it is Paul's. The men at the prison. Do they miss carpet? But that's an inappropriate question. Still, I'd like to tell them they're not missing anything.

Because I'm female, I have to teach the class with another person. My partner is Kelly, who is athletic and nice-looking in a wholesome way. She is nervous and concerned about her appearance. She puts on Chap Stick with strokes that flatten her pale lips and asks me if it's too glossy. I consider telling her the truth, that it doesn't matter, that the men will look at her mouth anyway, but I just tell her no, it's not too glossy. My husband told me I could teach dressed in a garbage bag and it would make no difference. One day she says to me after a class: "Mike, the one in the ponytail. I don't like the way he looks at you."

We never ask about the backgrounds of our six students. It might prejudice us. "I don't want to know," Kelly said, which made sense to me at first. But we find out anyway, learn that Ron, who always comes early and is quick to laugh, had been raised in a satanic cult, where he did a "lot of bad things." He's a born-again now and absently rubs the crucifix that dangles from his neck as if for good luck. Then there is Miguel, the one who keeps to himself. Kelly's right. If any of the men make me nervous, it's Mike. He seems to be the most aware of the fact that we are women. Jim always wears sunglasses, which he'll take off halfway through the class—startling me with his blue eyes—and an old denim jacket. He is handsome in an easy, rugged sort of way, the kind of man who could pick up a girl in a country bar. He likes to write about his days in San Francisco in the sixties, and I resist asking if he ever went to Gate 5, if he ever saw a little girl selling paintings on Bridgeway Street.

If any of them have raped or killed, we'll never know. Sometimes, during a class, I find myself thinking of the lies I've told in my life, the hurt I've caused because of weakness or apathy. I keep reliving the time in Lincoln City, high school, when I stuffed a stolen shirt in my jacket and walked, stiff with terror, to another store, where I wandered aimlessly until the woman who had seen me do it found me. A policeman gave me a ride home, and I was full of a shame so hot it seemed to burst from my very skin.

It's always tense when Kelly and I arrive. We know what will happen, because it happens every time. On the way to the educational building, we have to cross the yard. It is winter and the sidewalk curves a path through dirty snow. Later in the spring, the snow will melt down to reveal the bare ground, thick, sandy dirt. Thirty yards to our left is the gym. Men flock to the window and begin beating on it and shouting, their need both angry and desperate. The sound is muffled, a distant *poundingpounding,* the frenzy a blur in my peripheral vision. Kelly and I don't mention it, what we have caused by our presence. It is both power and powerlessness, and it is too big for us. We ignore it, which probably makes them crazier.

After the first time, I no longer look over at them. I focus on details, the white cauliflower of a hearing aid in a passing inmate's ear; tips of cigarette butts in the snow; a rabbit in the distance, bounding as if spooked. I no longer look at those men because it is enough to see them in my dreams, where sometimes they break through that window and hunt me down.

In the Event of a Riot
1. Stay clear of the altercation.
2. Remain where you are.
3. Find cover.
4. Keep a low profile. Avoid the appearance of observing crimes that rioters commit.

5. Look for a place to dive or roll if either authorities or offenders attempt to assault your area.
6. Do not attempt to negotiate. Your credibility as a negotiator is almost nonexistent.

Mike has written a funny story about his escapades at a juvenile treatment center. The others laugh when he reads it aloud—how once he had to climb a street sign to get close enough to read it and find his way home, he was that out of his mind. Miguel sometimes writes in Spanish. *Hace tanto tiempo que no estoy con una mujer.* ("It's been a long time since I've been with a woman.") I think he writes both what he wants me to know and not to know. Now and then, after reading Miguel's work, I dream in Spanish: *jugar* means to play. *Calor* is hot, *frio* is cold. The word for broken is *roto,* but it can be applied only to an object, not to a person. You could not say, for example, *Ella es una persona rota.*

I've seen a lot of fights in my life. Fights in grade school, high school, bars. I like to watch men fight, but I've learned this is not a good thing to admit. Mostly the fights are over quickly, after a rough push or a punch, before others hold them back. But sometimes they don't stop, and if whoever I'm with will let me, I'll watch to the end. Once, a boyfriend was jumped by two men, and later, bathing him, I blotted away the blood with my tongue, catching whatever was left.

I watched while one man broke my mother's nose.

With another man, I would go to amateur boxing matches, bouts in the backs of gyms amid the smell of bodies and rubber and steel. I both loved and feared the thud and slap of fists on skin, the slide of bodies when they embraced to rest, the spray of sweat like heavy mist. Later, in bed, we echoed those sounds and it was good.

I secretly begin looking for a place to live. I read the classifieds in a coffee shop, then make appointments once or twice a week, in the afternoons. In each place I imagine myself there alone, free. There's just enough from the teaching assistantship to get by with a small studio, something near a bus line. Without Paul I wouldn't have a car. I tell myself it's a good idea to check it out, to see what's out there, just in case. In the meantime I've started confiding in another student, an attractive poet near my age, and I even bring him along to the apartments. He listens to my troubles and offers comfort. He assures me I won't have to be alone if I decide to get a divorce. Another friend advises me to start stockpiling some cash, hide it away.

That old saying, every bad person has a little good, every good person has a little bad. Why is it so easy for me to recognize the good in the men at the prison and so hard for them to see my bad? These men look at me with such respect. I wade through it—I could throw it against the wall.

I begin to meet with a counselor in an office disguised as a living room. I sit on a love seat and tell him my marriage is dying and that this might be all right with me. He wants to talk about my past, but I resist. One day I bring him pictures of me as a young girl, black-and-white shots of a kid in overalls, with an expression so innocent and open I feel something very near grief when I look at them. I want to grab her and run with her and keep her safe. But I don't tell him that; I simply hand him the photos as if to say, *Here is my life, this is all I can tell you.*

Our classroom is ordinary, except for the facts that we are locked in and a guard peers through the tiny window of the door every fifteen minutes. Kelly and I begin by assigning pages of Tobias Wolff's *This Boy's Life,* thinking the boyhood memoir will be the perfect thing. But Wolff's boyish pranks provoke no more nostalgia than *Love Story* would for a porn actor. We quickly move on to Jim Carroll's grittier *The Basketball Diaries.* Art, a new member to the class, especially likes this selection. Almost sixty, he's the most hopeful of the group. He writes in allegorical language about the plague of drugs and about King Heroin, who rode down on a black horse and slew all in his path, including, almost, Art himself. Art is tall as a young tree and just as slim, the sheen of his skin like stripped bark.

After the second class, Kelly and I put away our agenda because it feels cruel to impose structure on people who shower, eat, and defe-

cate according to a schedule. And so when Mike talks about his father at length, we follow the men's example and just listen, even
though in eight minutes this room will hold a Narcotics Anonymous meeting, and already half a dozen men are shuffling outside
the door. One man in a ski hat presses his face to the glass. Art enjoys talking to me about journalism after our class, in the brief minutes I have before I'm supposed to leave. "When I get out, I'm going
to be a cameraman," he tells me.

Volunteer Agreement
1. I agree to avoid undue familiarity. If an offender has a problem
   that is beyond the scope of my position, I will direct him to
   Staff.
2. I understand that persons under the supervision of the Department of Corrections have been convicted of criminal activity;
   that any offender I may have contact with may attempt to manipulate or take unfair advantage of me.
3. I understand that I am volunteering in a potentially hazardous
   environment and that I could be taken hostage or injured.

I think about the men in my class when I should think about
other things. At the store, I wonder what they would want for dinner. I wonder if they've ever had kalamata olives or cabernet from
the Carneros valley. I imagine us all at the Snake River with a cooler
of beer and the Rolling Stones on the radio. I wonder if they are allowed to have music in their cells—or anywhere. But I can't bring
myself to ask. The question might offend them, as if my knowing
that they were denied something so basic would be humiliating. I
drive away in the evenings and turn up the radio. When I know the
words, I sing.

The prison staff thinks I'm safe, that I'm protected by the gates and
keys and bullet-proof glass. Everything is controlled and locked and
monitored, yet it makes no difference. The danger is something I
could pick up, like a weapon, and make my own. It is something I
could open myself to, like facing a hot wind. Some turn away from
it. Men I know on the outside don't like that I volunteer at the

prison. It makes them uneasy. They think I'm foolish, naïve, and they look at me and shake their heads as if they know something I don't.

What would they say if I told them that, over the past few weeks, I've come to know these felons more intimately than my own husband? Not physically, but on the page. I've read about their lives, their mistakes, their lovers, and their crimes. I write comments on their manuscripts, small clues to let them know me.

At home one night after class, I stare at myself in the mirror, then undress and stand there naked. It's been weeks, maybe months, since I've been with Paul. I touch myself and it feels strange, new, and my body shivers. Later, alone in bed, I think about Mike from class, wonder how his hair would feel fallen over my face, wonder what his neck smells like. He wrote about losing his virginity, and I responded in the margin, *My first time was like this, too.* For days, until the next class, I live in fear that he's told someone. Kelly notices and asks if I'm all right. I tell her, "I think I'm coming down with something."

Finally I find a studio, cheap and clean, and put down a small deposit. Later, on the way to class, I meet Paul at a restaurant, one we've gone to a few times, where we know what's good on the menu, where the waitress is familiar. I tell him there, at the table over coffee, that I'm leaving, and that I've found a place and plan to move in that night. My voice trembles and sounds hollow to my ears, and I find it hard to look at him, at this man who is doing the best he can.

I hope the practical details will make it sound real and logical; we've both been so unhappy for so long. Here is a solution: I'll leave. But he's stricken, his expression filled with disbelief, his face white. He just stares at me. I wish he would yell, humiliate me, hurt me, as if only that could lessen this pain, this guilt.

I know immediately, even with the memory of Paul's face filling my mind, that something is different tonight. Ron, who is the first one to class, is unusually subdued; it's clear he doesn't want to talk. The others come in one by one, and there is something in their exchange of glances that Kelly and I can't decipher, something in the way Jim sits back in his chair, arms folded over his chest, in the way Mike holds his pencil with his whole fist. I think about the boundaries in each of these men, where they lie.

Class has just ended when the shouting begins, and I'm not surprised, only relieved at the inevitability of things, the way tension can't last—the way skin bleeds when cut. Kelly and I are nearly at the copy room, on our way to make copies of the inmates' manuscripts so we each have one. She runs to the door and looks back at me. *"Come on."* I hear the instructions in my mind: *In the event of a disturbance, lock yourself in.* She whispers through teeth: *"Get in here."* The commotion is coming closer, but I don't move, instead I take a step away. Her words are faint, as if they've traveled a great distance—through water, through the cement of a wall. Deep inside I feel as if a key has clicked in a lock, things are falling into place. I shake my head at her and turn away from her wide eyes, toward the end of the hall, where a crowd has formed quick as cats to a struggling bird. Inmates huddle around two men in a fistfight. Tense, hunched with hands on knees, the onlookers gesture and yell as if they are a part of it, and soon they will be.

More inmates from the gym stream down the hall and surround me. For a moment it's hard to breathe, but, finding a rhythm, I move with them as if we're one. For a split second I think of a concert I was nearly crushed in, trapped in a crowd close to the stage, pushed and pulled, fighting for breath, and then feeling a stranger's firm, insistent erection against my hips—

The hall is narrow and long. The shouts of three dozen men ricochet, and in the chaos the only view can be seen through triangles of elbows, slits between legs. Two men scramble and punch and kick, the linoleum floor is smeared with blood now. A lip is split, a nose flowing blood, a shirt torn in a harsh swipe. The air is thick with the smell of sweat and skin and something else—fear and anger and lust. The bigger one tries to pin the other, is kneed in the groin and falls back clutching and cursing. It doesn't occur to me then that the guards, who run down the hall, their heavy boots hammering, can't see me. They're yelling, but it only adds to the shouting. I'm dimly aware of my fear, but the excitement is electric, overriding it. I can't look away from the riot. In their rawness, their rage, what secrets of men will be exposed?

One of the fighters, darker and slighter, grips the other's hair in his hand so the man bends to his knees. His head is arched back, mouth gaping, white throat exposed and bowed like the backbone of a small, pale animal. Another man from the crowd begins kicking the man on the ground in the side before he is grabbed and pulled down also.

Then the shoving begins all around as the guards push through, and I duck, but not fast enough, and I am slammed against the wall, where I sink to my knees and cover my face. Later, I will think back and it will come down to a feeling, the feeling one has just before jumping off a cliff's edge to the river below, the giddiness that clings to any moment where there's an edge.

After the guards have taken the men away, Kelly and the supervisor will look at me, their faces transparent with confusion and disappointment. And something else, something very much like repulsion. The kind that comes from seeing something contrary to nature. As if they'd seen a dove catch a mouse and gut it. Or witnessed a young girl expose herself in front of strangers. I see myself in their reflection: I have committed a crime, I have run to something women are supposed to run from. But I can't explain myself to Kelly or my husband or the supervisor, who orders me to leave and never return. They wouldn't understand that this fight had to happen, that I'd been waiting for it, that the tension of the past weeks couldn't last.

Driving away, I feel spent, shaken. The road hurls itself into the distance and keeps veering left and right, and it's an effort to drive straight. I'm going home to a new place now. When it begins to rain, I pull over and begin to cry. Not far off, there is a woman in a farmhouse, standing at the warm light of the kitchen window. She must be looking out at her own reflection, and does it please her? For a strange instant I think she could give me the answers, but the rain runs in rivulets down the glass, and I cannot see her face. There is only a shifting clarity.

21

Karyn's Story

"Joelle?" It was my father, calling from Maui, his voice a warm streak so strange in my Spokane studio. It was rare to get a call from him, and I wondered what was on his mind. He asked me about my new place, school, the weather. I could hear the quick inhale of a cigarette, and for a moment I was there with him in his living room on Maui, just the two of us talking about the day, the way we used to. But he was too quiet, his voice strained.

"Karyn's dead," he said. And he told me that his niece, my cousin, had been murdered by her boyfriend. In the kitchen of their Las Vegas apartment, he had stabbed her to death in front of their two small boys.

That was all my father could tell me, and after a few days of numb shock, I eventually went about my life as if her death didn't matter, carrying it like a silent, dark secret whose weight I felt only at certain times, when distractions fell away. And at those moments, the horror of it was like an assault of its own. I'd think, *It can't be true.* But somewhere inside, I knew it was true, and more—that the story of Karyn's killing began years before, in Hawaii, and maybe even when we were still children.

After my divorce, I realized I had to find out what had happened and why. Her death was somehow connected to my life, and the way I lived it. I researched the murder, ordering court files and back newspapers; I called the lawyers who'd handled the case. Then I booked a flight to Las Vegas. My friends and parents were wary—my father told me to "let it alone." But I couldn't. For me, Karyn's murder was an untold story, a ghost that haunted the living.

In July I flew to Las Vegas over an ocean of reddish desert, of craggy sand, rock, and alkaline dirt; it was the surface of a ruined planet. And I recalled a word, *caliche,* the chalky crust of calcium carbonate that forms on the stony soil of arid regions. On the mountains, trees grow thinly over the sand, like a close beard on skin. Houses cluster below, tiny toys in an otherwise empty sandbox. Walker Lake, a man-made reservoir, is a steel-gray puddle from that vantage, the only source of water you'll see.

After an hour the plane banked over the city of Las Vegas. The landscape there is flat and slopes in the distance into the Red Rocks hills. From above, the theme-park casinos look ridiculous: Treasure Island, New York New York, the tiny gleaming sphinx—miniature cartoon creations one could crush with a thumb. I wondered what Karyn thought as she flew in. She was raised in Kailua, minutes from the ocean. All her life she lived close enough to walk to it, to hear the waves late at night. Below me, the only water was fenced in—thousands of swimming pools squinted at the sky. The only green: tiny squares of lawn, smooth curves of golf courses.

Las Vegas had become a prime destination for Hawaii's residents; travel agents and airlines advertised Vegas as "the place to play." Hawaiian Airlines, one of seven major carriers with the Honolulu-Vegas route, flew more than three hundred people daily from the islands to the oasis that is Las Vegas. One wondered what the attraction was. The Strip, Las Vegas Boulevard, is not much more dramatic than Waikiki's Kalakaua Avenue. The same young men in shorts thrust coupons in your face (LIVE! NUDE! TO YOUR DOOR! CALL 24 HOURS!). The same tourists, wearing new sandals and T-shirts, studied their maps behind black sunglasses. But there is the gambling, of course.

The heat is where Hawaii and Nevada come together and then

most starkly part. The relative humidity in Las Vegas in July, at five P.M., is only 14 percent, versus Kailua's 80 percent. Dry heat stresses the body more than humid heat. In the plane it was cold, the air-conditioning too high. As we landed, I wondered why Suki brought Karyn and the boys to Vegas. I knew she felt oppressed by his family; they lived with ten other adults and children in one small three-bedroom house, and she couldn't make a move without it being commented on. Suki's small yard-maintenance business was floundering, and Karyn, a hairstylist, knew of a job at a beauty salon in Las Vegas. In any case, this move was a chance for a fresh start, a new throw of the dice. Maybe, with just the four of them, life could be good, she could relax.

I arrived at two P.M. The pilot had told us the temperature was 110 degrees. As if to close itself off, my skin tightened. For the next three days I felt swollen with unbroken fever; lotion evaporated like rain on pavement. When I returned to my car and sipped my bottled water, it burned my lips. This is a place that can age you, dry you up like old canvas. Heat here can drive a person to drink or to kill. I walked by a bush and touched the leaves, and they crumbled in my hand.

It could have been me, I kept thinking, though I recoiled from the thought. If family stability is any indicator of future success, Karyn should have had it made. Her father and mine were brothers, but they couldn't have been more different. Though he loved me deeply, my father was the alcoholic, the gambler, the one who couldn't keep a job, who couldn't hold a marriage together. Most of his old friends wouldn't have anything to do with him, or their wives wouldn't let them. My mother did her own share of drinking, of running from man to man and city to city. Home to me was the furniture we brought with us from one house to the next—the curve of an armchair, the nasturtiums photograph now faded to sepia, the wooden Buddha with the missing hand. Money was always scarce.

All through her childhood, Karyn lived with both parents and her siblings in the same comfortable house with a pool. Her mother doted tirelessly on her children: her family was her life. Karyn's father, my uncle Gerald, graduated from Princeton and was well known in Honolulu as a successful businessman and an excellent golfer, popular at the local country club. People still say of him: "He was a good family man." It was easy to assume that his children would do well in the world. Large, ruddy-faced, he had the look of a man who was well acquainted with the good life. He bailed my father out of debt many times, helped get him jobs, pulled strings. Though Gerald was handsome only from a certain angle, he was quick to smile and to laugh, and no one could believe it when he died of cancer so young, in his early forties.

So when Karyn "went local" and rejected her family and the path it pointed her to, it didn't seem right. If anyone had predicted which brother's daughter would get into trouble, they would have picked me.

Reading the newspaper articles, I wondered about the spelling of her name, of the *Y* in Karyn. It used to be Karen—maybe she changed it, a small gesture of independence, the kind only a young girl would make. I shortened my name to Jo when I was fourteen, liking the crispness of it. Karyn and I shared our experience of living in a small town by the ocean, hanging out with boys who were going nowhere, who drove beat-up cars and smoked pot and played the guitar or drums. The kind of guys who hold your arm with one hand up high, near the shoulder. Guys with tattoos still fresh on smooth skin. Life is simple with them. You know where you stand; the boundaries are clear. Feminine and masculine become rigid identities. There is no ambiguity, and in that life, fights are part of the deal. In that world even a black eye can be a badge of some kind: you're mine. It's a simple life, and one she must have clung to.

Years later, I would watch a film in which the lovers were constantly fighting and then making up in bed. I remember thinking, *Yes, I want it rough so that I can reach that stage where control is no longer something to hold but something to let go.* But it was more than that. I wanted clarity, too, to know how much a man might want me. There is such a fine line between anger and lust. I've been lucky. The men I've chosen haven't hurt me. One man put his fist through a cabinet and split a bowl in two, but he hadn't the capacity to direct that punch at me, or so I believed.

Well into my twenties, I gravitated toward men who wanted to possess me, secretly enjoying their jealousy, the way they glared at other men who watched me. I wanted them to fight over me. Nothing could be more thrilling, it seemed to me. My mother and my aunt Kathy had been involved with this kind of man during my childhood. My mother still has sinus problems from her broken nose. Kathy fled one night and changed her name because she knew her husband would kill her if he found her. Yet she had loved him. The yelling, slamming of doors, the drama, all of it was familiar to me. I remember one time hearing my mother and a man fighting in their bedroom, the slaps and cursing, the sound of broken glass. Then silence, and then low laughter. Later that night, they couldn't stop touching. And when I heard that Karyn had a possessive boyfriend, even a violent one, I thought I understood why she might stay with him.

When my father called and told me she was dead, I learned that she'd been killed on my birthday. I want to say I'm sorry, but I don't know to whom or for what.

Just off Paradise Avenue lies Manhattan Street, a tidy road bordered by endless apartment complexes. Karyn, Suki, and their two young sons lived in Sunrise Village, a modest row of gray condominiums trimmed in green and topped with hacienda-style tile roofs. Small palm trees dot the property.

Here they lived their tenuous existence. She worked at Supercuts, a hair-salon franchise, where she specialized in short hair. She was good at it; over the years in Hawaii, she had built up a clientele, regulars who would pay twelve dollars instead of eight to have Karyn as their stylist. More than once she had won the "most requests" contest for the island of Oahu. "She loved her job," Karyn's sister, Lori, told me once. "It was the only time she could be social, could be herself."

Suki worked in the kitchen at the Casino Royale. In a deposition a year later, he stated that he worked "from seven in the evening to seven in the morning. It was killing me. We never saw each other and I guess we started growing apart. I came home and she would be leaving to her job and I had to watch the kids." Since the move, he had lost twenty pounds and slept no more than four hours a day, and he was often drowsy from medication he took for the epilepsy that had plagued him since infancy. Except for their acquaintances at work, Karyn and Suki had no friends. They liked to drink rum and Cokes and Long Island iced teas and smoke pot—the evidence sheet shows that more than seven of the trial's seventy-one exhibits were photos of marijuana and paraphernalia: *Exhibit 36-B: Blue bowl, ashtray, and green leafy substance, offered and admitted.*

From the ground, I looked up at apartment 48 and tried to imagine the stairs running with blood, the way her sister described it. "They don't clean it up for you," Lori said. An old man came out with his dog. He told me he'd lived there only a year and a half. Not wanting to upset him, I didn't ask questions. The woman downstairs looked me over carefully. She remembered what had happened and told me there had been three other deaths in the complex since then—two murders and a suicide. I wasn't really surprised. The headlines in that day's *Las Vegas Sun* reported that Nevada, for the second consecutive year, was ranked as the most dangerous state, with violent crime up by nearly 40 percent. I took some photos and left.

One year after they'd moved to Las Vegas, Karyn was packing to leave Suki for good. The evidence sheet lists three photos of Karyn's packed suitcase. Although she'd talked of leaving for years, she'd told her sister that this time she meant it. Suki had finally crossed the line: two weeks before, he had struck the older boy, who was two. The next day, she left for her mother's in Utah, quickly and without telling anyone. Over the next few days she talked by phone with Suki frequently; he pleaded with her to come back, promising things would be different. But she knew it was over, that she would return only to pick up her things, give notice at work, and go back to her mother's with the children. Suki didn't quite believe it— they'd been together twelve years, and he'd heard this many times before. A psychiatrist later reported that "as long as they were talking, sleeping together, and arguing, Suki believed that Karyn would change her mind."

Back in Las Vegas, during the two to three days before the murder, Karyn often called her mother and Lori; in the background, they testified later, they could hear Suki yelling at Karyn that he would kill her if she left. Everyone was beginning to take his threats very seriously, except perhaps Karyn herself. Her mother had said to her days before, "For God's sake, watch your back."

I last saw Karyn two years before her death, at our grandmother's funeral. I hadn't seen her since before I'd entered the University of Hawaii, even though we lived only thirty miles apart. Off to the side, she and Suki stood leaning against their rusty pickup truck. He was slight, dark, what people in Hawaii would call a local, a term referring to any mix of ancestry: Hawaiian, Portuguese, Asian, Filipino, Samoan. It was the first time I had seen him, and I felt shy, uneasy. He was skinny, his face impassive, and he kept his eyes down. Next to him, Karyn seemed large and white; they were an incongruous pair. I could see no trace of the mischievous teenager I had known, the girl who would pop her bubble gum in my face, who'd taught me to do a back dive, who'd given me a bracelet of shells. I remember the unbidden thought: *She's let herself go.* She was only three years older, but she looked hard and tired, and though she'd always been plump, she'd gained even more weight. She gave me a defensive glance, and I steered clear. I was surprised to see her clutching a tiny bundle to her chest. I hadn't even known she was pregnant.

Karyn and Suki met at Lanikai Beach Park on the east shore of Oahu when they were both nineteen. Her sister, Lori, disliked him on sight. "He was scrawny and shifty-eyed. Controlling. And he wore these disgusting mesh shirts." After six months of dating, Karyn moved in with him, sharing his bedroom at his father's house. Along with his father, they lived with three of Suki's siblings, two of whom had their families with them. They lived in Waimanalo, only about forty-five minutes from busy Honolulu. It's a beautiful part of the island, still mostly untouched by tourism. In this neighborhood, families extend into the dozens, and everyone knows everyone. And because of that, haoles—white people—stick out. Like Karyn.

When I was in college, my friends and I would drive through this area on our way home from a day at the pristine beaches of the North Shore, and as we slowed through the little town, I always felt conspicuous. Sometimes we might stop at the grocery store for a soda. This was a mildly adventurous thing to do, like crossing a busy street against the light, and we did it in that spirit, casually and yet with all senses on alert. It was an unspoken thing. In these stores you could buy SPAM and Chinese crack seed and *ahi poke,* a kind of marinated raw fish, by the pound. The cement floors were always grimy with dust, cool against our bare feet. Resting in the shade of the awning outside, young kids would sit on the bench, swing their slim brown legs and slide glances at us. For the most part, we were ignored. I knew I was being tolerated, that my presence was for the most part unremarkable, possibly amusing or annoying. Although we were haoles, we were also kamaainas—not tourists, which elevated us slightly.

As far as our family was concerned, Karyn had emigrated to another country, with its own laws and even its own language. And so, on Easter Sunday and Mother's Day, we gathered without her. It was never clear if she couldn't make it or just didn't want to. But it seemed there was always something vaguely shameful about Karyn having "gone local."

My father said he thought she decided, on some level, to gravitate toward the local world after she twice failed the entrance exam to Punahou School, a grueling academic test and oral interview. Punahou, where Dad and his brother, Gerald—Karyn's father—went, is the best junior and senior high school in Hawaii and the oldest private school west of the Mississippi. The tuition is high enough to ensure that Punahou's student body is mostly haole and Japanese students, and virtually everyone in the graduating class goes to mainland universities. It was understood that all four of Uncle Gerald's children would go to Punahou, even though it meant almost an hour commute from Kailua. He could afford it. Karyn's younger twin brothers, Tim and Todd, and her older sister, Lori, all got in. So did my brother Ken.

Because I didn't move to Hawaii until halfway through my senior year, I didn't apply. I went to a public school a half mile away, where, because I was a mainland haole and disliked by many of the locals, I spent my time trying to dodge the insults and laughter that flew my way in the halls. I took so few classes there that I was able to leave by lunch; it took me months to make friends.

Karyn ended up going to a different public high school, where she fared much better than I did. I was so stiff and shy that no one wanted to know me. But Karyn, born and raised in the islands, knew how to fit in, knew how to speak pidgin English, something her father forbade her to do at home. He knew there was a time and place for it—on the golf course, at the store—but he didn't want his daughters to speak it anywhere. "Why don't you go out with the haole boys?" he'd ask Karyn. Many locals—but certainly not all— live within a patriarchal system, embracing a macho culture. Lori said her father wanted his girls to avoid the "real" locals: the ones who worked blue-collar jobs because they couldn't, or wouldn't, speak proper English, for example. "I don't want to say he was prejudiced. He just wanted the best for us."

While Gerald was alive, Karyn stayed away from local boys, for the most part, but she wouldn't stop speaking pidgin. Pidgin could mean survival. I knew this, too. Adopting local ways was the only way to make it through public school, and besides, I loved Hawaii—I wanted to fit in like my brother, who could speak fluent pidgin when he wanted, slipping between dialects like a slalom skier. I took hula dancing; my brother taught me to surf; I badgered my father into buying me some sundresses and plastic slippers. But the key, I thought, was to speak pidgin. I listened carefully, studying the quick, lilting chatter of my classmates and local people on the bus, in the stores. At home in front of the mirror, I'd try out phrases and intonations, such as "You like stay," the *stay* dropping down two notes because in pidgin, questions don't lift at the end to the expected higher tone; rather, they fall like stones, the last word left with the weight of an assumption. But it always felt false, as if I was trying on shoes that weren't just the wrong size but made for a completely different shape of foot.

One day I tested my pidgin on my father. He never spoke it, but like all haoles raised in the islands, he sometimes spoke with the pidgin accent when it was convenient. All my life I'd seen him use that accent to gain the confidence of a certain local at a store, or to show that he wasn't a tourist. Both he and my brother could instantly put people at ease. I wanted this skill; it would prove I belonged here, with my father and Ken, in these islands. I knew my father respected the local culture, the family loyalty, the lack of pretension and love of a good time, of food and music. I knew he'd rather spend an evening at a local bar than the finest restaurant lounge. But he never tried to be a local, to change who he was. As we drove down Kalakaua Avenue, I came up with an innocuous question and casually said, "You like go to the movies." According to the rule, I let *movies* rest low. Even as I said it, it sounded horribly stupid to me. I had clumsily switched into a new, false identity. I saw myself suddenly as my father must have: ignorant. My face burned.

I sat tensely while my father considered the implications. I imagined that a future was presenting itself to him: his daughter falling into the local world, sleeping with muscled local boys with tattoos of Hawaiian warriors, going not to the University of Hawaii but instead to a beauty school in Kailua, like Karyn, or a correspondence school in Honolulu, getting married young and having too many kids. All this he would have contemplated in seconds. He could have answered my question with "Yes, let's see a matinee," which might have been a surrender to that glimpsed future in some small way. But he said only "So, I see you know how to speak pidgin." I shrugged, mortified, and didn't speak for the rest of the ride.

I actually think she wanted to leave the white world long before the Punahou School rejection. She was the middle child, sandwiched between a pretty blond older sister and her handsome younger brothers—twins, no less, so attractive they were finalists to star in a Doublemint gum ad campaign. Karyn, always overweight, with buckteeth and eyes too close together, seemed the odd one out even as a child. In one family portrait, when Karyn must have been eleven or twelve, Lori stands over the twins, hands comfortably on their shoulders, and Karyn is separate from them by several inches. Against their blondness and perfect smiles, she looks like a distant relative, or maybe just a friend.

I doubt Karyn chose to go local in the way one might choose to change her identity, the way I briefly did—unnaturally and desperately. It must have been the easiest course for her. A rhythm she stepped into. In the local world, she was a haole, and a local boy with a white girlfriend was granted grudging respect, often outright admiration. Being haole was a complicated identity: it could be dangerous in the wrong places, but it could also be a great advantage. There were so few haoles at her school that Karyn was a prize. She was always noticed by the local boys. And it didn't matter that she wasn't educated or very pretty.

I heard rumors from my father about Karyn. He told me of the endless threats, the beatings, of how Suki would park outside the beauty salon where she worked and watch her through the window to make sure she didn't go outside to "check out guys." He didn't allow her to wear shorts, and never a bathing suit. At the beach, he made her wear pants, which she'd roll up before going into the water. My father told me of the time Karyn and her Supercuts coworkers locked themselves in the back of the store while, outside, Suki threw himself bodily at the plate-glass window again and again, and finally hurled a giant rock with both hands, shattering the window. But I'd quickly try to forget it. It was as if we were discussing something fascinating but distasteful. I gradually figured out that this was another of those problems that is to be whispered about but to which there is no solution.

But late at night, almost ashamed to admit it even to myself, I'd wonder at the passion of a man who would try to hurl himself through a window for you. To see a man so lose control, that idea haunted me. I wondered what it would be like. Of course, I never thought he would kill her, but then I didn't see the daily arguments; she didn't run to my house, as she did to her sister's, in the middle of the night; I didn't have to hear him crashing through the bushes outside, hear his cries of "I love you, Karyn!" I didn't see any of it, but I don't take any solace from that now.

This killing had been a long time coming, regardless of whether anyone chose to see. Lori said to me, "The saddest thing is that it didn't surprise us." And so now our family is steeped in regret—for her, for ourselves. This wasn't a random murder, for which we would rightfully feel a deep rage, but one in which we all felt somehow implicated, as if it were not just Karyn and Suki's story but our whole family's. In fact, I've often thought of the grammar of the phrase "Karyn's murder"—as if it were somehow something she owned, something that was hers. Other languages lack this implicit accusation; in French you would say "the murder of Karyn." But in the end it's still the same. She's gone.

Over time, I've come to understand the mechanism of shame, which has within it a dark seed of self-recognition. Even though I was young, how could I have ever envied her life? Did I need a man's love so much? And with the shame comes guilt; how can you blame another for taking a path you might have taken yourself?

The evening of May 8, Maria Jordan, a police officer with the Clark County school district, was watching TV with her nine-year-old son and two of his friends. Around seven P.M., she heard a violent banging on the floor above her, coming from apartment 48. She would testify later that it sounded like two sumo wrestlers. In his opening statement, the deputy D.A. quoted her as saying it was "very violent, and a pounding, pounding noise."

Jordan was fed up with the months of fighting, which had only intensified during the last few days. Putting a coat over her nightgown, she went upstairs to tell them to shut up. When she got there, she heard children screaming and a man's voice yelling. There was no response to her first series of pounds on the door, but there was a response after the second. Suki opened the door, wearing brown corduroy pants and a white T-shirt with purple sleeves—all of it covered in blood. He said to her, "I snapped. I screwed up."

Behind him, through the front door, she could see Karyn lying on her back in the middle of the kitchen floor, a butcher knife protruding from her throat. Jordan ran downstairs, yelled to the boys to get under the bed, and grabbed her off-duty gun. Back upstairs, she leveled the gun at Suki and told him that she was going to take the children. The two-year-old boy had blood on him and was crying hysterically on the floor. She grabbed the boy and ran downstairs, commanding her son to "Get this kid under the bed with you." She then returned upstairs and pointed the gun at Suki, who stood motionless while she grabbed the eight-month-old boy.

When Suki was taken by the Metro officers, he told them, "Shoot me," and "I'm sorry."

Karyn had been stabbed forty-two times: four wounds to the front of her neck, seven to the back of her neck, five to her back, ten to fifteen to the chest. The strikes to the chest cut her larynx, so she could not scream. There were five slashes on her face and mouth. One in her side was delivered with such force that it pulled a portion of her viscera back out through the hole. There were numerous defensive wounds on her hands and arms.

An expert in forensic evidence testified later that Karyn fought for her life and was initially stabbed as she stood. There were at least two, possibly three, attacks, three different series of blows. Based on the position of her body and the way the blood had drained from it, she was at one point standing or leaning against a wall, facing it, and either by her own physical movement or by the action of others, she was turned so her back was to the wall and the knife was then driven into her neck, where it remained.

I look at the documents and plaintiff's exhibits numbly, feeling sick with it. It's a list of photographs, a gallery of her death, spread out on my living room floor. But I also feel an unnerving sense of relief. There is the proof. Maybe this is like finding a body that was missing for years. Until it's found, you live with a quiet anxiety, on the edge of minor insanity even, because it is just too crazy, too unreal to comprehend. This couldn't have happened in my family; it's all some kind of sick joke. But then the evidence—documents, transcripts, letters—the evidence comes in the mail to your home. The language so simple and clinical, handwritten by a clerk: *Exhibit 51-A control sample, blood-like substance.* All in black and white. *There is the body,* you think. *Now I can go on.*

I don't know how Karyn's death affected the others in my family. It taught me that I'm stronger than I think, and that I was luckier than Karyn—a little bit smarter, a little prettier. Maybe it's that simple. Most of all, because of her I'll never long for the feel of a tight grip on my arm. Maybe she's saved my life.

In the end, this is only my version of what happened to Karyn. Any of my cousins, my brother, Karyn's mother or children—each would tell it differently. Who is to say which of the stories is the truth? I prefer to believe that all our stories are true, that their currents join together and flow along the river of memory in which Karyn lives on still.

22

Johnny

That was the winter we kept each other warm. Until I met him I drifted like snow through the frozen, dark world of Albany, New York, where I was pretending to be a dedicated Ph.D. student. I huddled in classes, dreading the long bus ride home at night. The weather was worse than Spokane's, and I didn't have a car or money to buy one. I piled on layers of sweaters and coats and wrapped a scarf around my face.

Johnny was in two of my night classes, sixties literature and poetics. An English major, he was hoping to get into the master's program the following year, so he'd gotten permission to take some graduate classes. I thought he was too young for me, though he was older than most undergraduates. I was twenty-nine, and I guessed he was twenty-two, maybe twenty-three, but he intrigued me, and over the weeks I began to look forward to his presence in class. I liked to watch him, his slouch, the outstretched legs. He was wearing the same thing every time I saw him—a plain T-shirt and wrinkled brown or khaki pants, black overcoat, faded blue baseball cap over his wild, curly black hair. Deep black eyes to match. He was Italian, and he smoked Marlboros outside in the snow during class breaks.

He was nothing like my ex-husband. I pointed him out to my

friend Sarah when I saw him walking one day across the campus. "Look at that guy from my poetics class—don't you think he's sort of attractive?"

Sarah, who was dating an older professor, dismissed him with a wave. "He's too young, too sheepish-looking," she said. "You can tell he wants to be Tom Waits or Lou Reed, one of those damaged poet-musician types. And look at that goofy walk."

It was true; with his long legs he loped along, and he had big feet. He reminded me of a dog with very large paws. But that was kind of adorable, I thought, though I didn't say anything to her. And what was wrong with Tom Waits and Lou Reed? I watched him write in his notebook, his head bent forward, his neck a soft shelf, an invitation for my hand to rest there. The sight produced an ache in me, as most vulnerabilities in men do. From his comments in class I knew he was bright and sensitive. Whenever he realized I was watching him, he'd look down quickly, embarrassed. Then he'd look up again, see my eyes still on him, and squirm a bit in his seat, take long breaths and look with concentration through his notebook. Once I realized the effect I had on him, I took advantage, enjoying his nervousness. But I knew I'd react just as he had if he decided to look at me the same way.

Johnny seemed like someone who would plunge into love, fall headlong without looking back, who would hold me all night in that place of oblivion, that dreamspace where nothing is real but the press of your bodies. This was exactly what I was looking for.

It was clear that I would have to initiate a conversation. One night, during a break, I told him I liked a comment he'd made about the writer Richard Brautigan. From then on we'd talk a little after a class, and finally he invited me to a concert, someone I'd never heard of, Robyn Hitchcock. Johnny insisted on buying my ticket, which was flattering because I knew he was as broke as I was. It was snowing that night, with warning of a blizzard to come, but neither of us wanted to cancel. I dressed carefully, knee-length skirt over dark, warm tights, a heather-gray turtleneck sweater. He picked me up in his messy car, though he'd cleared my seat, and shocked me when he handed me a ten-page poem he'd been working on for a couple of days. It was partly about me, he said, and I was touched—the idea of his writing these pages that very day. Reading it later, I was relieved to find that it was good.

We drove north for an hour through the furred snow of the highway, the windows steamy inside. Cars swayed by opposite us, their headlights dim as lanterns in the storm. The world tightened around us, and I imagined we were in the middle of a white sea. We felt reckless, abandoned, and when the car skidded, we'd shriek and then laugh—so what if we tempted fate? I couldn't think of anywhere I'd rather be than here, on the edge of some wildness, of love.

Only a few cars were parked at the roadhouse. Inside, about two dozen people sat around listening to the concert, which had already begun. We found a couple of stools by ourselves at a high, round table and let the music wash over us. We each had a beer, and after a while Johnny took my hand, and he said, a little embarrassed, "I have an erection." His candor surprised me, but I looked down at the mound in his pants and said, laughing, "You sure do." This seemed to ease things, now that we had acknowledged the lust between us. We relaxed and enjoyed the music, which was incredible—the singer didn't seem to care about the storm, about being in the middle of nowhere. He played for all he was worth for us and the handful of people, this winter, this tide of snow waiting just outside to bury us.

After that night Johnny and I spent every minute we could together, and when we weren't together, we were on the phone. He used to call me from the bathtub to read a new poem to me, his voice hollow amid the faint sounds of lapping water and tiny splashes. I imagined him rosy-cheeked, hair sleek and wet, holding the ink-blurred pages. He lived in a studio apartment, on the fifth floor of an old brownstone. It was run-down, but I loved the details—moldings around the doorways and the border of the ceiling, the intricate shape of glass doorknobs, the built-in bookcase. After all the ranch-style houses I'd lived in out west, I found it romantic. We browsed the junk shops for posters and vases. He had a cheap futon bed with a slatted metal frame whose shape the mattress had taken; the bars were as tangible as ribs under a thick coat, and we had to shift our hips to settle between them.

He'd give me presents—a tape he'd made for me, a used book that I'd been trying to find for years. I'd surprise him with home-made ravioli and a bottle of Chianti when I could afford it. We wrote poems together, lying facedown, propped on our elbows, side by side on the bed. Late at night we sat huddled in coats and hats on the fire escape, drinking red wine and listening to the occasional sirens and the sounds of busy Lark Street below. He told me about the brother he had lost, killed in a car accident, and I told him about my dads, and he let me cry, not threatened by my sadness. I knew I could admit anything to him.

In the morning, when the sirens faded, we could hear the cooing of pigeons. It seemed we passed through a season in the night: at first it was warm, then hot after making love, the sheets flung back, our skin damp where it touched. By morning it was so cold that we clutched at each other, pressing everywhere, even our feet en-twined, as if we couldn't bear to be separated anywhere.

Often the moments between us were so purely fine and full of bliss that I fought back tears. *Who are you where did you come from?* I searched for reasons for his being here, being in my life. I thought he must be here to show me this was possible. I realized I had never loved anyone before—I was almost thirty and had never known it. Toward Johnny I felt grateful and something else: terrified.

When he was gone, I wore the T-shirts he left on the floor, run-ning my hands along my body through the fabric, his scent rising. We couldn't get enough of each other. Sometimes, after five, we'd have sex in the graduate-student office of the English department. Once, after we'd finished, we heard applause from some faculty gathering down the hall, and we laughed when Johnny bowed as if it were for us.

We tried to keep ourselves a secret for as long as we could. It seemed like a good idea—we had different social lives, and we doubted people would understand. I had a whole other life apart from him that he felt both intimidated by and disdain for—the faculty parties, the conferences I presented at. Johnny was barely hanging on; his teachers didn't like him or the strange ideas in his papers that looked more like poems than essays. His ten-page poem grew to fifty pages and became the bulk of his final project for our poetics class. The teacher, unnerved at all of the subtle references to me, said to him, "Does she know you're writing about her?"

It didn't matter. We liked being isolated—just the two of us, though we knew it couldn't last. My friends disapproved, as I knew they would when they found out. They said he and I didn't match—he was too young, just twenty-three, too awkward, a strange loner. Whenever they tried to talk to him, he spoke in non sequiturs. He refused to go to their dinner parties with me. They said I could do better, much better, and reminded me that I'd already done a master's and he was on the verge of flunking out of his B.A. program. What's more, he had none of the kinds of ambitions I did—of being a published writer and a teacher, of owning a home of my own someday. He thought all that was boring.

"I don't understand," said my friend Kris. "I don't know what you see in him."

And I'd say, "You don't know him. You don't know us together."

How could she? How could anyone? Their judgment only made me feel rebellious. I was attracted to the unlikeliness of Johnny and me, the sense that, together, he and I were inappropriate. And yet sometimes their words would echo in my mind later, a white noise of doubt.

One weekend, after I got an unexpected check from an article I'd sold, Johnny and I drove to Woodstock for the night. We decided to take the back roads. We wanted to get away from the university, from Albany. The two-lane roads curved alongside farms and tiny towns, and we found ourselves inventing lives for the two of us. One of us would point to a house or cottage and say, "That's where we live—that's our home." Down the street I'd pick out a gas station where he worked and a florist shop where I worked, and Johnny would find a little restaurant and say, "That's where we go on Friday nights, where the cook has a crush on you and gives you an extra-big serving of lasagna."

We laughed, but underneath there was a feeling of awe. These imaginary scenarios attracted and repelled us at once—we scorned the smallness of them, and the absurd idea that we could select the pieces of our lives like items off a shelf and hold them in our palms. Yet we also knew that we could live these lives we described in such detail, if we really wanted. We could go anywhere, keep driving all the way to Florida, to California. There were endless towns, countless variations. Life arrayed itself before us, fanning out its offerings like playing cards, and at times, it took our breath.

Not long after, I felt a shift in myself. I don't know when the fear started—it was so subtle, just a growing awareness that it couldn't work, there were too many obstacles. We were both at unstable points in our lives, and I could never quite forget that he still had most of his twenties to live through. He was still unformed, experience lay in wait for him. I'd see a younger woman and think, *It would be easier for you and Johnny.* The time we had together began to feel borrowed, as if I'd have to pay it back—as if I was in debt. I realized that underneath these excuses I was afraid of him, of the power he had over me. The more deeply I felt for him, the weaker I became. He could hurt me so easily if he chose, and whatever door had opened because of him began to close. It wasn't long before I began to use it—the unlikeliness that had first attracted me to Johnny—as an excuse to leave him.

Some mornings, while waiting in the cold for the bus, I'd think about my mother and of all the men she had left, or who had left her. What were the reasons, what sense did they make? Did she ever truly love any of them besides my father, so long ago? What I wanted to know was whether she ever left out of fear, fear of being hurt, of being left behind. But she was on the other side of the country, and her regrets couldn't teach me anything; they couldn't help me. Whatever mistakes we held in common, I was making my own now.

·   ·   ·

More and more, it began to bother me that Johnny thought tragedy was beautiful—his poems were full of images of doomed love. I accused him of being more in love with the romance than with me.

"What would you do if I left?" I asked one day as we walked through Washington Park.

"I'd write poems about you. You'd be my muse, or the memory of you would be my muse."

The tension grew between us. He tried to make me jealous, I suspected both because he saw me slipping away and also for the drama of it. One night we rented a movie, and he said of the actress, "I hope you don't mind, but I really like Hispanic women." I glared at Johnny, not because he was trying to provoke me, but because when I imagined him with someone else, she would now have a face, a body. I would know the shape of her legs, the curve of her waist. There was some twisted relief in this: our life apart would also seem more real—it would be easier to let him go.

As May approached, I retreated further from Johnny. I had applied and been accepted to the University of Iowa, where I could get another master's instead of continuing on with the Ph.D. program at Albany. Johnny and I didn't talk about whether he would go with me. I went to coffee with a friend's brother, but it was just flirtation. Then I met another Ph.D. student, a linguist. Although he rarely bathed and sat in the lotus position for two hours a day, he was my age and on the verge of a promising career. I downplayed my involvement with these others, knew they were only distractions, made excuses for why I wasn't home. I knew I was hurting Johnny, and I hated myself for it. One night I didn't return his call and went out to play pool at a bar around the corner from my studio. I saw him out on the street, ducking behind a parked van. Looking for me. I don't know if he saw me. I felt guilty and ashamed and also pissed off. I thought: *I want you to adore me, but not that much. You're ruining any chance we have.* Though in truth it was me, not him, who was the culprit.

The next day he showed up and sat on my bed, and he described to me how to make a homemade bomb. I told him to quit talking like that, that he was scaring me, and he laughed. His eyes were cold. I told him to leave, but he said no. I opened the door and said, "Get out." He walked over to the door and stood close to me and said, "I know what you're doing. You don't have to run away from this." *Yes I do,* I thought.

I think about him still. I loved him, and though I tried to deny it, my love for him had a hold on my heart and crushed it into something I wasn't sure I could control. We might have made it if I'd been willing, if I'd been ready. He made me feel free and strong and beautiful, and I loved what happened when we were together. The way my head fit into his shoulder as I lay with him all night, listening as the city finally quieted. I left him. I left him before he left me.

•

23

The Winemaker

I used to watch my father watch other women. I'd sit by him in the bars and restaurants where we met, and follow his eyes. Lids half lowered as he sipped his drink, speculative and discreet, the sweep of a glance if he found a woman worth considering. As if he were absently fondling the idea of her but it didn't matter whether they met.

This is the way Stephan looks at me at the café where I am working for the summer: a subtle appraisal, a small gesture of interest. I notice that he watches me with other customers, and I smile more brightly, though I'm tired and hot. He orders a club sandwich, an iced tea, and chocolate cake. I like that, the cake. Most people don't order dessert at lunch. It could mean he's frivolous or indulgent, but what I know it means is that he has time. Good-looking men— it's nice when they linger.

I pause at his table to ask if everything is all right, refilling his tea from a pitcher. I let him know certain things about myself. He approves, I can tell, of my master's degree, of my being an English teacher, though he's surprised I still waitress during the summer months. Although I tell him, "It's just part-time, it's fun," I do it be- cause I need the money. Before he leaves, he invites me to a party at a nearby winery on the weekend. An annual June celebration. I ask him if he works there, and he says: "I own it." He runs out to his car to get his business card, and another waitress says to me, "He's fine, yeah, but he's an ass." She's worked here a long time—she's seen him around. She likes me. It's clear what she's doing, but I've never heeded warnings before, though I know I should.

Because I have plans, I don't go to the party, but I think about Stephan over the weekend. I remember his brown eyes, the mischief in them, the desire. Later, I call and apologize for missing his party. We talk for a few minutes, of the highlights of our weekends, and he asks me to dinner.

He takes me to his winery, high on a ridge in Sonoma, the terracotta courtyard circled by palm trees and waist-high vases of red bougainvillea. Wisps of steam rise from an outdoor Jacuzzi, partly hidden by ferns. Here he often entertains guests and clients on summer nights, and he shows me where caterers stand before haunches of large animals on giant rotisseries. We stand above the whole of the valley flung there like an enormous pastoral tapestry, and it's as if this land is his—all of it and everything beyond—and he is offering it to me.

But before the winery we go to a new French restaurant that's been well reviewed. I let him order and sit in quiet surprise as he selects four hors d'oeuvres, soup, main courses, desserts. He's brought two bottles of his own wine, a zinfandel and a chardonnay, which we drink in that order. He discusses each wine and its fine attributes, one finger pressed lightly on the bottle. The dishes come steadily, each more elaborate and exotic than the last; bowls and plates and glasses crowd the table and people begin to notice. In the candlelight, the colorful sauces and glazes shine like rain-soaked flowers. We eat creatures from Easter scenes—rabbit and duck, lamb and quail. Stephan loves meat and adventurous dishes, and I try to forget my affection for animals.

I wear a knit dress with thin straps, and a push-up bra. By the time the crème brûlée and chocolate-almond cake arrive, I am fairly drunk. I can't believe how much we've consumed, the ravaged table. We flirt and joke, avoid talk of anything serious. He says, "I want to kiss you," and does after we stumble outside to his black Mercedes. We search for yet more dessert, this time poached pears in cognac, from another restaurant. He orders them to go and brings them out to me in the car, where we unwrap and eat them with our hands right in the parking lot. Syrup splashes on my left leg, and with a finger, Stephan sweeps it up and licks it.

He drives fast, curving through dark back roads of vineyards, stereo blasting, and I laugh as he sings out loud. I stick my arms through the sunroof and wave at the stars. At the winery, we climb into the Jacuzzi and he peels off my bra and panties in the water, and we have sex, then again a while later on a chaise longue in the court-yard. The night air is still warm, and the heat held by the terra-cotta tiles feels good against my bare feet, my hands. It is slow, the way he tastes me here, and there, and there. He takes little bites and holds my flesh between his teeth, lightly, as if I'm something to savor.

Through the haze of sex and wine, I think of the other women who must have been here before me. The faint pangs of shame threaten like rain in the distance, coming steadily closer. I know it's too soon to be with him, that he'll disrespect me, that this will cost me. But I know even more that the act of sex will bind me to him, that I'll want this again and again. I think to myself: *Another man's arms.*

Later, still naked and damp and laughing, we make our way bare-foot down a trail to his wine cellar, cut into the slope of the hill like a well-hidden cave. There, thousands and thousands of European, South American, and Australian wines are arranged neatly as a li-brary of books. He is so proud, I can see, of this fabulous collection, of this nude woman as witness. The climate-controlled air ripples our skin, and we press against each other as he opens a bottle of bur-gundy made from grapes grown in France before I was born.

I fall into his life that summer, into the rhythm of meeting him at the winery after my shift, then driving the hour to San Francisco with him, where we dine out and dance and stay in his Pacific Heights house, and then the next morning, tired and subdued, we drive back to Sonoma. He likes to put the car on cruise control and lift a socked foot one and then the other, into my lap, which I massage as we coast over the golden hills. I stop calling friends; the letters I've vowed to write stay unwritten.

Much of the time we end up with his friends in the city, sometimes a dozen or more. He likes to show me off. And when he puts his arms around me at a club or party, I feel warm inside, like I am claimed, wanted, a part of. He is proprietary but somehow absent. He carries a satchel of wine the way an athlete totes a gym bag. He buys dinner and drinks for people who love to let him, and the checks often amount to more than I make in a month. The chef comes out to greet us because Stephan's wine is good and expensive and he always leaves some behind for the staff.

At the bars I look around and fight the dizziness—there are women everywhere, it's a sea of women anchored by men. Most are younger than I am. Unlike me, they don't show their fatigue yet. Groomed, their clothes stylish, toenail polish matching fingernails matching eye shadow—all the half-moon spaces of their bodies colored in. In the bathroom, I see dark circles under my eyes; I pinch my cheeks to rosiness. I've waited tables all day on the deck, in temperatures in the nineties, and my feet swell in their high-heeled sandals. I tuck them under my chair. I fight feeling interchangeable—if another woman were to sit in my place, would Stephan notice? Suddenly, as if I'd caught the image in a window passed by, I know that Stephan will sit here in a few months, perhaps in this very seat, with someone else.

He tells me nothing about his feelings—not his desires or fears or ambitions—and he doesn't want to hear mine. We never talk about the future. We live in the perennial present, satisfying our needs as they arise, for entertainment, food, sleep, sex. I find myself thinking that I should know better. I should know better by now.

Stephan is thirty-nine, with beautiful skin, smooth and almost moist in its suppleness, like the skin of a grape. He is careful with his appearance and uses cosmetics for men, by Clinique. Yet he is not dainty or openly vain, just clean. Before sex, Stephan likes to gently wash me, as if it were some sort of absolution. We shower together and take long bubble baths after our nights out, sometimes when we return at dawn. He soaks yellow washcloths and wrings them out over my body. The water washes away the wine, the doubts. I am cleansed of any wrong.

I like his hunger for me. He takes me in the kitchen, in the hallway, in the elevator; on the way to dinner his right hand wanders over my body and under my skirt. All night, leaning close, I can smell myself on him. He does the most intimate things to me and I to him. This is the way of our communication. When we make love, I forget everything: the coldness that comes after, the way he pushes a barrier of blankets between us, tells me to keep to my side. Instead, I memorize the way he looks at me, how he stops and lies still inside me, his face in my hands, as we hold each other's gaze between kisses. This is when love happens, I tell myself; this is what gets me through the night.

We live this double life, the sweetness and intensity we spend on each other's bodies, wanting only to give and give the best pleasure. And then, out of bed, the banter, the surface talk. I tell him when he isn't nice, which is quite often, and he laughs.

It takes me weeks to realize that all the friends and the wine dilute any friction. I discover there are other women; sometimes they call, and with a clenched gut, I overhear their chatty, affectionate voices on the answering machine. Stephan leaves for golf and sailing trips and doesn't call, though I've never asked him to. His house is very neat, dustless, new-smelling—a maid comes on Tuesdays and lugs her burden of supplies from room to room, wiping away my presence, our lovemaking. And yet I find small reminders of others: a red barrette behind the toothpaste; a phone number on a torn napkin in the desk: Julie. When I confront him, he waves it away, and I admit that I will do without love just to feel wanted. I am like one of his wines, worthy of a connoisseur's attention. Coveted. But I know that he'll move on, adding to his collection, never satisfied with what he has.

One night I make dinner for him, a gourmet meal for which I shop an hour and spend three days' worth of tips—fresh Chilean sea bass, portobello mushrooms, artichoke ravioli, fresh orange daiquiris. I cook barefoot, wearing a white slipdress, while he watches and sips his drink. The food, the wine, the sex: this is how he stays alive, how he staves off the fear that ultimately he is alone and afraid, and I think, *This man was once a boy.*

Later, I tell him that I love him, though I realize it's not true. But I want to. That should be enough—that I want to. And he puts his finger on my lips and says, "Be quiet." This is not what he wants to hear. In the middle of the night, I stand by the window overlooking Buchanan Street, and the shutters cast bars on the wall and across my cold body.

There are no teary goodbyes when I leave for Iowa, where I'll be teaching fall classes the following week. Stephan walks me to my car and tells me to keep in touch, though I know we won't. It takes me three days to drive to Iowa City, the California sun receding farther with each highway marker I pass. I let my mind find him in fantasy, in a beautiful home where we cook for each other and sleep nestled like kittens. There have been others like him, men who have burrowed within themselves to a place I could never enter. Men who long ago shut themselves off, just as I have.

We speak again only once, months later. I'm shocked when Stephan phones in the middle of the night to tell me his father has died of cancer the week before. For an hour he talks steadily, almost hypnotically, in a tone both bewildered and reverent, of the funeral, the music, the elaborate flower arrangements and all the people who came. He's never spoken like this. He tells me about his father for the first time—I hadn't even known he was sick. I know he must be desperate to call like this, to open up like this. Maybe he's called all the women he's known, awakened them from sleep all over the country, and talked to them about his father. Maybe we're all he has.

I listen, let his words pour over me, imagine him half a country away, holding the phone closely, sitting on the edge of his bed. I want to talk to him about the valley, the way it looked to me that first night, the vineyards a vast, dark blanket below, how the wineries upon it lit up to the night, beckoned like faraway cathedrals, each offering some kind of salvation.

Instead, I try to comfort him, to offer words of kindness, even of love, though I can tell it's too late for that now.

24

San Francisco

When he calls from New York and says he'll be two days late, when he offers his apartment to you, tell him yes. He sends his keys with a note, *Make yourself at home.* And *You can sleep in my bed.* You think about those words for a long time. You're nervous about being in his apartment without him. He barely knows you; you've had only that one dinner.

You have no trouble finding it. You feel like a spy or a thief, coming to his place at night. The key slides in as if it were yours. You walk through his apartment and it seems as if he's just left. His clothes lie in laundered piles by the closet, papers loosely stacked on a camelbacked couch, and this pleases you, the casual order. You smell him everywhere, his smell as much a part of the air as the light. Even the washed towels hold the scent of his soap. The pictures of him—playing soccer, the Dartmouth jersey he's wearing, the poised kick and fierce expression. And the others, the artsy black-and-white, the one at the piano. It takes confidence to display oneself like that.

Walking through his rooms, you catch glimpses of yourself, seeing yourself as he will see you in two days. It is startling, how different you look, as if the mirrors' surfaces hold imperceptible curves that reveal to you for the first time the truth of your appearance. Is this what he sees? He said he thought you were beautiful. You know you are beautiful only from certain angles, and soon he'll discover this, too.

Everything so still and quiet, a sense of waiting about the place. You look at framed photos of smiling strangers at events you never attended. Those things that are important to him. Pieces of his life lie scattered like clues—receipts and ticket stubs, an empty wine-glass, a *Newsweek* spread open on the bathroom floor. You are afraid of what you might find, traces of a girlfriend, evidence of an interest in something unsavory.

You run your finger along the spines of his books, admire the selection; open cabinets, see the cups and plates arranged so nicely. The sunblock and aloe sealed in a plastic bag, sand still clinging to the necks of bottles. He saves pennies in a small dish and chews the ends of his pens. The way his shoes line up (neatly paired), the colors he chooses to wear (you wouldn't have guessed all the blue), the candles half-burned. His bed is made. In the medicine cabinet sits an unopened box of condoms.

You begin to feel at an advantage. He had said on the phone, chuckling to soften it, "Be sure to *bring something short, something slinky.*" So you hang your short, slinky dresses beside his clothes in the closet and think, *I could do anything here.* Put on the cream slip dress you brought for him, the deep plum lipstick, pile your hair and drink his good merlot on his bed. Cab to a fine restaurant and sit at the bar. You could say to the bartender, the tanned business-man beside you, *Can you believe it, I've been stood up.* Take someone home to the apartment. If you made love with another man in his bed, whose body would you smell as your face pressed the pillow? Whose name would you call?

You stand in the dark and watch people through the blinds, but you see shadows mostly. You want to see people bathing or undressing, you want to witness an intimacy. You are not used to the city, to these apartments stacked like great white blocks with no space between them. You lived here, as a child, but you remember nothing like this. You hear people walking above you and talking below you.

The woman next door—she whistles. If you turn on the lights and open the blinds, you could be seen doing something ordinary, like making tea or folding clothes, writing a letter.

And what if you were naked, standing there? Would someone watch you? Are you less alone if someone is watching you?

Later, you lie on your side on his bed and observe your body in the mirror above the dresser. This is what he will see: your face, round shoulder, curve of breast. You wonder where he will touch you first. How he will touch you. He will certainly pull the blanket from your body to look at you.

He said, *Go ahead, sleep in my bed.*

You like to reveal yourself slowly, if at all: you've always preferred sleeping at your lovers' apartments and sleeping alone in yours. You like the idea that your smell and the outline of your body remain in their beds after you've gone, that they could not sleep without you even when you'd left. Even when they washed the smell of you from their sheets, the memory of your weight, the small of your back against their stomachs, the hardness of your heels would linger while they slept. And you loved equally to come home to your own bed, free of them and anything they wanted.

You don't spend all of your time in his apartment. You walk the marina streets and the fog follows you like a shadow, like something you could get lost in. The boutiques of Chestnut and Union show you everything you've ever desired. Each reveals more of what you've missed, what you couldn't afford. In Victoria's Secret you eavesdrop on a couple who disagree over the shade of nightgown. She wants white, but he prefers the wine.

Your mother used to carry you through these city streets—she'd take you to concerts and festivals and to the corner market for fruit. You keep looking for something familiar, a stairwell or window frame, a slope of roof that might signal a place you once slept, that might have been your home for a little while. When you and your brother were kids, this is the neighborhood your father drove you through in his taxi. You know this city is important to who you are, and it lies open to you, like the man's apartment you wait in. But you are a stranger in both.

When you first met, he said, *I want to know all about you.* You don't believe him, you've heard that before. You remember the familiar, distracted gaze. He listens, but his eyes flicker over your face, your lips, your throat, as if your voice were merely an accompaniment, your body the main event.

Isn't your desire for him enough—what else would he really need to know? That you're divorced, that you will never pierce your ears, that you like it from behind? Or that you prefer to wear black, to make love to certain songs, to take naps on dark days? But what about this: what if you told him about your father, about the things you've stolen, about what it sometimes takes to get you through the night? Would he want to listen to your fears, to hear of the images you can't forget—the blind man you drove by one night, the way he just stood there alone in the rain, your frightened brother reaching for your hand, your mother's face collapsed in grief as another man left?

You remember men who loved you more the less you revealed. As you pulled from them, they reached for you. You let them love your body, opened it to them as if that was the only gift you could give, that and the memory of it when you were gone. What you have brought them to, such painful hope of nothing. He's not afraid of you, but he should be.

The two days blur, and you sleep and you walk and you wait. He comes back the second night, and after a dinner of delicate Japanese food you lie in bed together for the first time. And after, he'll hold you from behind. His semen on your thighs, the wetness dried tight and thin as faded scars.

He will ask you, "Are you awake?"

And because you are, because sleep seems loose as mist, you say, "Yes."

"Are you comfortable?" he asks. "Is my arm too heavy on you?"

It is heavy—solid and too warm—but you tell him, "No, it feels good."

He'll wonder if it was lonely without him, and you don't answer. Somewhere over the bay a foghorn blows, and it's a sad warning, too late.

"Admit it," he says. "You were lonely."

You answer him with a question: "Did you ever wonder what I would do?"

And he won't know what you mean. So you say the question in a different way, "Just, did you ever think about me here, alone?"

He answers: "It makes me feel closer to you, somehow, that you were here. I liked coming back to you."

Remind him that he doesn't even know you.

And when he says, "But I *want* to know you—tell me something about you, anything," say to him, "Here's one thing I can tell you: this is the city where I was born."

25

Plumeria

One summer when I was five, my father taught me to make leis, and for many years that was how I began and ended my visits with him in the islands. We'd sit on the lanai and spread out hundreds of fragile plumeria flowers, light as cotton and much softer, threading them like popcorn on a string. The plumeria, though round like a daisy, has only four to five wide petals, and no center of pollen, just a small opening where the petals unfurl from the stem. The eye of the needle was wide enough for lei thread, waxy and strong and thick. Before the missionaries introduced needle and thread, my father told me, the Hawaiians used strands of banana bark as string and stiff grass blades as needles. We tried it once, peeling strands from the banana tree in the front yard and threading them through stiff blades of grass, laughing at our clumsiness.

Hawaiian grass *was* stiff. Each summer it took my feet until mid-July to toughen up enough to walk barefoot on it, carefully avoiding the giant African snails that skimmed their way across the yard with their spiraling shells. Still, I wondered how the early Hawaiians could make the beautiful leis my father described with just grass and bark. Lei making is delicate work. Each blossom has to be a certain distance apart: too close and the stems can tear from pressure; too far and the string might show between.

We began with the gathering, taking a basket into the backyard, and if there weren't enough flowers on our tree, we searched the neighborhood for the rest. Everyone's yard had at least one plumeria tree. They were everywhere. They grew in the oily dirt of alleys, in strips of grass along parking lots and bus stops. From a distance they looked like giant bouquets, sturdy trunks topped with dark green leaves and clusters of bright blossoms. Sometimes we walked a while to find my favorite, the ones with the yellow centers, which smelled sweeter to me than the pink or pure white. Pitched on my father's slim, broad shoulders, I plucked flowers at the base with a quick twist, each coming off with a soft snap at the seam. The simple ease of this seemed to suggest that they were meant to be picked in their prime, not left to wither, curled and brown.

I knew, though, that picking them was unnatural because of the white fluid that bled from the exposed stem. Thin and sticky, the sap dried quickly to a tacky residue on my fingers, like wet candy, only not sweet at all. In fact, my father often warned me, it was poisonous and could cause blindness if it got into the eyes.

As I grew older, my father would tell me about Hawaiian history as we made leis, the giant mound of flowers more than a foot high between us. The smell, pure and sweet as warmed honey, seemed to envelop us, and to this day I only have to smell one plumeria flower and it all comes back again—the cool blossoms tumbled over my bare legs, the rustle of mango trees in the wind, my father at peace beside me.

He described the steamer ships that came to Honolulu in the early nineteen hundreds. As soon as the lookout on Diamond Head spotted an arriving ship, word was passed, and lei makers lined the dock to sell greeting leis for the visitors. My father once showed me an old black-and-white photo of dozens of Hawaiian women sitting cross-legged along a wall, each with an enormous basket of flowers. The women wore wide-brimmed hats, faces hidden as they strung their leis. What intrigued me the most was the tradition of throwing one's lei overboard as your ship returned home: if the lei drifted back to shore (as it usually did), it meant you would come back someday.

. . .

My father had also learned as a child to make plumeria leis, from the trees that grew around his family's cottage. He lived with his parents and his older brother in Makiki Heights, a white neighborhood of Honolulu. Their cottage sat in a small corner of my grandmother's cousin's lavish estate. Her cousin had married a Cooke, a woman descended from one of the Big Five families of Hawaii. These were fabulously wealthy and powerful kamaaina haoles whose ancestors were missionaries and merchants, shipping captains and plantation owners. That made my father's family "calabash" relatives of the Cookes—related by marriage.

My father grew up in the forties and fifties knowing he was a "poor relation," a term never spoken but understood nonetheless. For parties and holiday dinners, he and his family dressed in their best and then walked over the lush acres of lawn, dotted with monkeypod trees and bushes of Tahitian gardenias, to the "big house." There, Japanese servants in white uniforms served cocktails on silver trays, while my father played outside with the other children.

My father and his brother—like their first cousins in the big house, Molly and Blake—went to the private elementary school Hanahau'oli, a feeder school for the elite Punahou system. Hana Haouli means "happy work" in Hawaiian, and its curriculum focused on creativity and self-expression. At these schools my father and Gerald were given an education that rivaled any of the East Coast boarding schools, and their classmates were the most privileged people in Hawaii—the rich Republican haoles. Outside of this world, the non-Caucasians of Hawaii—the Asians, Portuguese, and native Hawaiians—saw the whites as a homogeneous upper class. This was still territorial Hawaii—Hawaii didn't become a state until 1959. Unlike mainland America, whose awful legacy of slavery led to legal segregation and hostile relations between blacks and whites, Hawaii's racial and class system most closely resembled colonialism, with the peaceful coexistence of races and a segregation policy that was unofficial but still very real.

Yet that rich haole world had its own clear hierarchy, invisible to the outside eye, and my father was fully aware of it. His family had no money. His mother was a schoolteacher, his father a manager at

RCA. But what my father lacked in pedigree and cash, he made up for with charisma, good looks, and a sharp wit. His IQ had tested at 150, and he had an almost photographic memory. His grades were terrible, but he aced his tests. It was common knowledge among his friends that he was brilliant, though he never flaunted it, and he dated any girl he wanted—the Punahou girls liked his self-deprecating charm, his offbeat sensitivity. He was one of the most handsome boys in school: tall, blond, and broad-shouldered, with big green eyes. The guys liked him for his sense of humor and for the subtle rebellious streak running through him.

But at the end of every dance and party and fancy dinner, my father went back to the small cottage on his rich cousins' estate. He had the constant sense that he was both inside and outside of things—that it didn't matter if he was smarter or funnier than his cousins, because such qualities would get him only so far. He would never be quite good enough.

I'm looking at a picture of me with my father when I was a baby and he was twenty-seven. It was taken in 1967 on Kauai, where we lived for a while before my parents divorced, a time I can only imagine. My father, who is grinning and holding me, wears pink and orange madras shorts. I'm startled to see the clearness in his eyes. He stands on a seawall, and behind us is the ocean, so shallow it isn't blue but a light green—it will be in this water that he teaches me to swim. He will hold me at arm's length and blow into my face, surprising me into holding my breath, and then dip me in and out of the water.

What strikes me most about the picture is the way he holds me, one arm circling me against his side like a satchel. This is the way he always held me, as if he carried me everywhere, so naturally was I a part of him.

Much of my childhood was spent flying across the Pacific between Hawaii and the mainland, between my father and my mother. I loved flying. The stewardesses gave me playing cards, pinned pilot wings to my shirt, and, when I was tired, propped me up with small pillows. My grandmother always met me at the gate in Honolulu.

In those days passengers still disembarked on the tarmac, and I loved the drama of descending the narrow stairs before the crowd of waving people behind the rope, their hair and clothes wild in the heavy wind. And beneath it all, the smell of flowers in the warm, humid air. My grandmother, wearing a bright-colored muumuu, would give me a plumeria lei and a candy lei made of Life Saver rolls, wrapped in pink or yellow plastic netting. A ribbon was tied between each roll, and for the first few days I would untie a ribbon each day and release a roll to share with my cousins or other children on the beach or in the neighborhood.

After a week she would put me on a small plane to see my father on whichever of the islands he was living at the time: Molokai, Kauai, Maui, where he would meet me with a plumeria lei he had made. Usually he was living near the beach, where we spent most of our days. We'd pack a lunch of Chinese crack seed, frozen strips of mango, guava juice for me and my brother, and beer for our father. Sometimes he brought a pitcher of gin and tonics, and I'd suck on the limes. My brother and I swam and played all day, building castles, and I would sit on the moist, warm sand and hug my knees and lick the tops of them, and at times I thought I could taste the sun.

He doesn't swim anymore, but my father was an expert bodysurfer then. I wasn't very good at it and preferred to sit on the shore, my little brother beside me, and watch our father angle into the curl of the wave, arms close to his sides like a dolphin. I'd hold my breath, not letting it out until he emerged yards away, shaking his head free of the water with a grin. Later, my brother and I would bury him in hot sand to his chest. We even made a sand table for his drink.

When we weren't at the beach, my father took us to the Maui country club. He wasn't an official member, but most of his friends were, and he met them there to play golf and drink and gamble. He'd drop me and my brother at the pool, where we'd swim all afternoon, often until sunset, and when we were hungry, we just signed my father's tab at the snack bar for delicious, greasy hamburgers and ice-cream drumsticks for dessert. If I didn't see my father for hours at a time, it didn't matter. He'd come and check on us, watching us perform our tricks in the water. And I could almost always find him in the clubhouse bar. I'd wrap a towel around me and wander into the cool, dim room where my father would be sitting with his buddies at a table littered with drinks and ashtrays. My father would order me a Shirley Temple and set me on his lap, where I stayed as long as he'd let me. I loved to hear their easy banter, the loud laughter.

I know now that my father was deep in debt. He bet on golf and horses and football—it didn't matter. When we went home from these afternoons at the country club, Kaui, his wife and Ken's mother, would go through his pockets after he'd passed out, hoping he'd won something, knowing he wouldn't remember if he had, and she'd steal what she could for groceries and bills so the electricity wouldn't get turned off again. She'd known he wouldn't be a good provider since their wedding day in Reno, when he lost almost two hundred dollars at the craps table—all the money they'd scraped together for the marriage license and the honeymoon motel and the gas back to San Francisco. But that was 1969 and she was young, with only a vague idea about life and responsibility. She married him anyway because there was something irresistible about my father, something that made you want to take care of him even as he made you laugh, the way he made you forget, for a while, that life was actually quite hard and unforgiving.

My father taught me that *lei* means "love"—they have always been given to the Hawaiian gods as a sign of devotion. I learned that the act of giving someone a lei originally symbolized a child putting her arms around a mother or father. Forming a circle with his arms, my father showed me the motion. And like the word *aloha,* which means "love" and "hello" and also "goodbye," the lei is versatile. Nowadays leis are given to people for graduation, birthdays, retirement, even to commemorate a new building.

When I was a little girl, you had to either make a lei yourself or go to one of the lei makers in the tiny shops tucked away in the alleys of downtown Honolulu. When we needed something special, my father would take me there and we'd walk up and down the noisy, narrow sidewalks until we found a shop we liked. He'd barter with the owner and come away with a bright orange rope of ilima and strands of sweet green maile, which we used for weddings and luaus. The lei makers were considered artists, and the leis hung from the walls in dazzling colors and patterns, the smell of thousands of flowers nearly making me drunk. I always asked to carry the leis, cradled in woven baskets or ti or banana-leaf wrappers so the flowers could breathe.

Today, packaged leis hang behind refrigerated glass at convenience stores and airports. Flower girls in sundresses and high heels weave in and out of bars selling from their baskets of leis, the small white pikake, the rosebud, the white ginger. Most drugstores offer plastic and silk flower leis, leis of candy bars strung end to end, and even strings of miniature bottles of liquor, some alternating vermouth and gin to create a "martini lei."

I often wonder how my father started drinking. His parents liked to golf at the Oahu country club and liked to drink in the clubhouse afterward. My father was a caddy at the golf course and hung out there all the time. Did his father give him a taste of his gin and tonic in the clubhouse, or let him sip from his glass of cold beer? Maybe he and his cousins stole rum from the liquor cabinet of the big house. By the time he was in high school, like everyone else, my father smoked cigarettes and drank like a grown man. I can imagine him in his letterman's jacket, his bleached blond crew cut and tanned skin like something out of a Beach Boys video. He and his friends would go to parties, to the beach, for drinks at the Outrigger Canoe Club at the edge of Waikiki Beach, listening to Johnny Mathis, Elvis, the Platters, and from Hawaii, Kui Lee and the Surfers.

But my father drank harder and more than most of his friends, and when other people might have heeded the wake-up calls my father got, he ignored them. He flunked out his freshman year at Duke because of the drinking. That summer back in Honolulu, he had two car accidents. He hit a woman at a crosswalk in Kaimuki when the sun blinded him. She was okay, only had minor injuries.

The newspaper article reported that he'd admitted to having a couple of beers at Sandy Beach, where he'd spent the afternoon. And on a humid August night, he dropped off his date at her house in Kaneohe and then almost died on the way home after passing out at the wheel and crashing into a guardrail, his bones broken, blood seeping through his white dinner jacket.

He spent the fall recuperating from the accident and taking classes at the University of Hawaii. It wasn't until the spring semester that he returned to the mainland for college, this time to the University of Oregon, where he would fall in love with my mother that autumn, telling her on their first date as they walked through the campus in a rare snowfall that he would marry her.

By the time I entered high school, I had become just another anonymous passenger on the plane and, like everyone, received a chocolate-covered macadamia nut for dessert on my tray, garnished with a single purple orchid. It seemed to me that the orchid, a hardy flower, was chosen not for its smell but for its durability. The plumeria, on the other hand, is delicate and begins to wilt soon after touching warm skin, as if for its sweet scent it has to sacrifice endurance. I loved its fragility and felt protective of it. On my trips back home to Oregon, in my lap I'd carry the plumeria leis that my father and I had made—one each for me, my mother, and my brother Dace. It never occurred to me to wonder why we spent hours making leis that would not last more than a day or two.

My lei hung in my bedroom window. When it faded to a soft brown circle, I'd toss it into the Columbia River that flows west to the sea.

After I moved to Hawaii in the middle of my senior year, I took the required Hawaiian history class at Roosevelt High and fell in love with the language, the alphabet of only twelve letters, five of them vowels. The consonants seemed to come from the very earth—the strong *P* and *K*, the soft but full *L* and *M* and *N*, the subtle *H*. I liked to translate English to Hawaiian: *daughter* is *kaikamahine;* the flower that never fades is *pua mae 'ole.* I took hula dancing and listened to

Olomana and Henry Kapono. I wore a plumeria behind my ear. I wanted to understand Hawaii. Somehow this place was linked to my father, but now, I wonder, why did I think I would find any answers?

I think of what he told me once, about the statehood celebration of 1959, when he was nineteen. He said while other people were cheering in the streets, he was upset because he knew the real Hawaii was gone forever. He remembers walking all night, listening to sirens and bands, firecrackers and singing, a young man already wary of change. I sometimes wonder if he, as a white man, was aware of the irony of his nostalgia—it was the Americans, after all, who had overthrown Queen Liliuokalani and the monarchy.

One day I took a book of sketches and old photographs and walked around Waikiki, trying to reconcile the dated pictures of dirt paths with the busy six-lane streets, the thatched huts with glass-and-steel buildings breaking the sky. Glancing from the book to the world around me, the cabs honking, the crowd of tour buses, the jostling throngs, I felt completely disoriented. I turned a page, and under a picture of rice paddies and a lone coconut tree, the caption read: *This photo was taken on the site of what is now the Royal Hawaiian Hotel.*

In my thesaurus there are eleven synonyms for *drunk/drunkard*. In related concepts, *social group member*, there are over a hundred words, including addict, admirer, believer, coward, deserter, exile, failure, fan, friend, guardian, hostage, idealist, intruder, joker, lover, maverick, nobody, notable, original, outcast, pal, philanderer, rebel, sport, stranger, sweetheart, target, traveler, underdog, veteran, visitor, wanderer.

In order to understand the drinking, I have to understand my father. My mother told me once that to understand him, I needed to know about my grandfather's affair with a family friend, Gwen. For nearly twenty-five years, my grandfather loved this woman, wanted to marry her, but my grandmother refused him a divorce. She would have been destitute, her whole way of life pulled out from under her. The social network of friends at the Oahu country club, her women golf friends—all of it would have been over. And my grandmother must have known she wouldn't marry again. She had been forty-two when my father was born, and she was in her fifties and sixties during my grandfather's affair. And, too, she was homely—short and dumpy with bad teeth and wiry hair that turned gray early. She always looked out of place next to my grandfather's tall, stately good looks, his thick movie-star hair. She wouldn't give up him or the image of the wonderful family she had—a handsome husband and two talented golden sons. So she tolerated the affair, struck some sort of deal with my grandfather. I don't know if Gwen's husband knew. But for nearly three decades they were a foursome—my grandparents and Gwen and her husband—golfing together and going to dinner and drinks. My grandmother even went so far as to arrange a schedule with Gwen during my grandfather's last days, as he lay dying of cancer, so that they could trade off caring for him.

My father found out about it when the affair was only a few years old, when he was nineteen. The whole family had been in Seattle for a golf tournament that Gerald was playing in, and Gwen and her husband had gone along, too. One day, late in the afternoon, my father went back to the hotel to get something and found his mother crying in the lobby. He went to find his father up in their room, and when he opened the door, he saw him and Gwen together. The shock haunted him all his life.

He rarely talked about it, never to me, and hardly to my mother or his second wife, Kaui. He told you only the bare minimum, what he wanted you to know. But what his wives have said feels true to me: that my father never really recovered from this endless betrayal. It went on and on, year after year, this facade. He felt torn between his mother and his father—he lost respect for her, was ashamed at her passivity. And he was angry, though he also could see how his father could be attracted to lovely Gwen. I don't think my father ever forgave either of his parents for their weaknesses, for their choices. But, as my mother told me, he understood his father's—though what that understanding cost him, I can only imagine.

I believe he gave up a little in 1959, the year Hawaii became a state, the year he found his father with Gwen, the year he almost died in a car crash. So when he did go back to college—his chance to get a real career, like his friends, like his brother, Gerald—he didn't take it seriously. Instead, he read books and went to parties, and then he met my mother.

In the mid-seventies, my father was sober for eighteen months, and he loved it. He'd started going to Alcoholics Anonymous on Maui and then moved to Mill Valley to write his novel, where he eventually stopped going to meetings. But while he was going, he tried to get my mother to go to A.A., too—I still have the letter he wrote her. She remembers how surprising it was, my father who hated therapy groups and self-help trends, praising this twelve-step program. It *must* be special. She says it's because of him that when she was finally ready to stop drinking, in 1981, she knew where to go, to A.A. She says he saved her life.

Kaui told me something once that made me so angry I couldn't speak for hours. One night in 1975, when my father had been sober a few months, he and Kaui went to a friend's house for a dinner party. Being sober was a new and fragile thing for my father, she said—he'd quit a drinking habit that was over twenty years old. At dinner he told their friends. One of them, an old drinking buddy, laughed at my father's talk of sobriety. The man was sure it was a joke. Later, he went into the kitchen and got a plum that had been marinating in brandy, was soaked with it. He said, "Here, Ken!" and pushed it into my father's mouth. Kaui said my father turned white and got up from the table and went outside on the lanai. When she joined him a few minutes later, she said he was "just shaking."

After I calmed down, I realized I was angry at myself as much as that "friend," for my own behavior many years later, after my father had gone back to drinking. We met in bars all the time, and many times I'd order a beer, even if I didn't want one. It wasn't that he wanted me to—I doubt he cared. I did it because I thought it might make him feel less alone, that it might take the pressure off what we both knew, though we never talked about it. But mostly I did it for myself. If I drank, then it was easier for me to pretend that it was normal. I couldn't stand to face the reality of it, of watching him drink at a bar, watching him down half a beer at a time like some desert wanderer, starved and reverent.

I knew the truth. I watched, I joined in sometimes. And I never said a word. For years I've argued with him about his diet and his smoking, but I've never brought myself to confront the drinking. Many people have told me I should. They say, *Someday you'll regret it. What if he dies? How will you feel if you haven't said anything?*

When my grandmother died in 1992, we all made leis together—my father and stepmother, Suzi, my brother and me. It was the last time I saw my father make a lei. My grandmother wanted her ashes scattered in Kailua Bay, like her husband's. All afternoon we gathered plumeria flowers until we had hundreds of blossoms, many of which we left loose. The next morning the clouds hung low and gray over the water. Only a few *opihi* fishermen stood silently on the distant reef, as if standing watch for us. My brother and I and his friend Kimo, who would help us paddle out, put the leis and flowers in the canoe and nudged it out into water that reached our thighs. I watched the brown triangle of my brother's bare back as he paddled with long strokes, first right, then left, then right. We were silent except for the oars in the ocean, the softscooping of water.

Between my bare feet, her ashes rested in a koa-wood urn. We drifted to a stop and took the leis from our necks and dropped them into the water where they fanned out around us, rings of brilliant color, and then, handful by handful, we sprinkled the loose plumeria until we were surrounded by hundreds of colored petals. I poured my grandmother Tutu's ashes into the water, where they mingled with the pink and yellow and white petals, turning the nearest of them gray. Then we turned back toward the beach, where my father waited with his wife, my cousins, the minister. They stood in a semicircle, a lei broken.

I don't remember when my father stopped coming to the gate and met me instead in the airport bar. It might have been around the time the Kahului airport was expanded; most planes had to park at the end of the new terminal, which was too long a walk, my father said. It pained him because of his bad knees. I still haven't gotten used to his absence, and when I enter the gate I search the faces for his, even as I'm walking quickly through the crowd. At the bar, he is easy to spot: aloha shirt, jeans, thick blond hair, shoulders hunched over a drink. His body is tired and strangely frail for a man in his fifties, his height and blond hair suggesting a youthfulness that should be there but is not. He enjoys talking to bartenders—the airport bar is a favorite place. The respectability of it appeals to him. No one counts drinks.

He never forgets to bring me a lei when I visit. It's wrapped in chilled plastic, wet with moisture from the airport gift shop. After we hug and say hello, he puts the lei around my neck, then hands me the car keys. And we go home.

When I think of my father, I can't separate him from Hawaii. He is a part of these islands in a way I never was, never will be. But some nights here on the mainland, when the air is too thin and quiet and cold, I dim the lights and play my island music, the guitar and ukulele and Hawaiian words streaming through these rooms—and then the memories appear: I see my brother glide into the curl of a blue wave, taste the salt and sun on my skin and smell the sweet plumeria against my neck, and all the while my father is swaying to the song and everything is all right while he smiles at me so bright on some beach far away.

26

Ninety Miles from the Nearest River

Not even noon, and it's almost 100 degrees. My mother's car has no AC, so we've opened all the windows and sprayed ourselves with water bottles. Hot air pummels us, the rush of it so loud we have to shout to be heard, so we end up saying nothing at all. Just me and my mother and the Nevada desert.

This is insane, I think to myself. Why have I agreed to this? Maybe she'll come to her senses and we can turn back to Reno, go see a matinee in a dark theater or cool off with some ice cream. I look at my mother at the wheel, and the thought shrivels up like I've put a match to it. There'll be no turning around, I know.

She drives out this way about once a month to do a sweat with a random group of people, mostly Indians, on the property of a Cherokee-Mexican guy named John, who is the sweat leader. She describes the two pulpy scars that are spread over each of his nipples, mementos from a sun-dance ceremony during which hooks were ripped from his flesh by the weight of his own body. He lives in a trailer with his wife and daughter and three dogs a hundred miles north of Reno.

We arrive at two P.M., right on time, but for some reason the sweat has been postponed; no one tells us why, and it seems rude to ask. For hours we wait, sitting and then stretching out on towels in the sparse shade of a black locust tree, and the branches make shadows like claws on the sand. I stretch my blue cotton dress over my knees; it took us twenty minutes to find me something appropriate to wear. No shorts, my mother said. She's worked with Native American Indians for years as a counselor, and so I defer to her. It's been a long time since I've argued with her about what to wear to an Indian event.

We'd last done a sweat together almost ten years before, when I was in college, on the Colville Reservation in upstate Washington, where I spent a summer with her. All I remember is a terrible, dark heat and then the blessedly cool Columbia River, into which we stumbled when the last prayer was said, lingering on the bottom with sand and stones and quiet. But this will be different—this is the Nevada desert in August, and the nearest river is two hours' drive.

Around her short dark hair she ties a lavender bandanna, and then she rolls her sleeves high on her shoulders. Her light blue eyes are vivid against the frame of her tanned skin, as startling as wildflowers in the sand. Sweat tracks the sides of her bare face: she looks serious and pretty. Beside her, I feel content—it's a rare and pleasant thing to see my mother be still. In all my childhood memories of her, she is moving. I remember her quick steps, the brush of velvet skirts against my face. In pictures, too, she is forever animated, captured in midsentence, hands swiping the air, as if she could not be still even for the click of a shutter. I count back: it's been fifteen years since she's taken a drink. I want to tell her that I'm grateful, but it doesn't seem like the right time—for some reason it never does.

Instead, I listen as she draws designs on the ground with a stick and describes the animals that live around here. The Mojave rattlesnake, a very fast animal. The yellow-back spiny lizard and its rolling eyes. The western long-nosed snake, which is a good burrower, spending its daylight hours underground. *Oh God,* I think, shifting on my towel. "Don't worry," she says, laughing. "They only come out at night." She still wants to teach me, to fill the spaces in me that remain empty. She pulls out two eagle feathers from her bag for us to hold for strength during the sweat. "Just don't wave it at anyone," she says. During one of her first sweats she'd been chastised for fanning her neighbor. "These feathers contain powerful spirits—a person has to be ready for them."

She says this solemnly, in a tone I know not to question. She's so willing to believe these other people. I can imagine her: sitting on the dirt floor of the sweat lodge, generously fanning the panting woman next to her, the sweat leader's gentle reprimand, and my mother's head bowed in apology. She wants me to avoid her mistakes. It has taken her a long time to be accepted in this world. She's traveled the country, a white woman, teaching tribes about fetal-alcohol syndrome—I remember the nights she came home crying, exhausted. She had to learn about lowering her eyes, about silence, about keeping her voice even. It was suggested that she wear heels, to slow down her walk. She immersed herself in the world where the sweats, it seems, are the ultimate test.

Beyond us, the desert slopes and curves into the washed-out blue of the horizon, and in the distance, hawks circle intently. In the way that desolate places often are, it's beautiful in its simplicity. All afternoon, people mill around the yard and the desert beyond, shirtless men with hair caught in long ponytails, barefoot children, chickens. I lose count of the dogs, most stretched out in the shade of the house. Hunger presses vaguely. We've been fasting all day—no solid food—and in shame I think of the hunk of angel food cake I ate at the bathroom sink before we left, the hasty sweep of crumbs from the counter. After a while, I drift into a dreamless sleep, and sometime later, a little girl with a long braid wakes me up. The towel beside me is empty—I scan the property and spot my mother talking with Sue, John's wife, on the porch. She holds a small boy on her lap.

"Here," the girl says, handing me a can of soda, icy cold. "Thanks," I say, thrilled, and roll it around my forehead, press it to my throat. She smiles. She wears a *Little Mermaid* T-shirt.

"Is Carol your mom?" she asks. I tell her yes.

"She's really nice and makes the best bread."

I smile at her and nod; it's true.

"It is good the day is so hot," she says. "Because then your body won't be too surprised in the sweat."

Okay, I think—*that makes sense.* Fifty yards away, a bonfire blazes higher than two men, and waves of heat swirl and dance above; I can hear the crack and roar of it. This is the firing of rocks for the sweat. Even from this distance, I can feel its heat.

When it's time, the determination of which is a wonderful and mysterious reckoning in Indian country, we slowly start toward the fire and the sweat lodge, a large mound covered with blankets and tarps. It looks like a makeshift tent, absolutely uninviting on this blistering day. I'm supposed to crouch in there with a dozen other people? *This really is crazy,* I think, and yet I can't deny that I feel honored to be included. We pass a young Indian man, thin and tightly muscled, who holds a bucket filled with smoldering sage. Each of us slowly turns in a circle before him as he strokes the smoke over us, "smudging" and purifying us. Then the twelve of us sit on the ground outside the hut in a row: seven men and five women, about a third of us white. John, the leader, is small, wiry, his skin tight and brown.

"You must get down on all fours before entering the lodge and say 'All my relations,' as you enter," he says quietly, looking at me a beat longer than the others. "This will show your respect for our mother, the earth." My mother and I sit with our white knees folded beneath us. The sun presses down in the windless air and I can feel my thighs, slick with sweat where they meet. I lower my eyes and stare at ants in the dirt. Fat-bodied and black, they march in lines according to some mission, undisturbed by us. Once I glance at my mother, wishing she would wink at me.

John then lines us up—I'm separated from my mother by a large woman in a pink cotton dress. A dark triangle, where a blanket folds back, serves as a small door. I can't help but think of it as a symbolic womb, which makes me feel faintly nauseous. We crawl in one by one and sit in a close circle on the cool gray dirt around a shallow pit, where the fire-hot rocks will be. Instinctively, I breathe through my mouth. The air is thick with the press of already moist bodies, the odor of old blankets, traces of sage and musky dirt. I realize with alarm that I'm directly across the pit from the opening—as far from escape as one could be. If I panic, I'll have to scramble over people left or right to get out. The ceiling, two feet above my head, slopes to the ground close behind me, and even when I press my back against the blanketed wall, the pit lies only about a foot away. Space is so precious that unless I position myself at an angle, I can't sit cross-legged. I touch the ground. The dirt, soaked from years of human sweat, seems to melt between my fingers like chalk, like ashes.

With a pitchfork, the fire tender hurls a rock the size of a small watermelon into the pit, where it rolls toward me. Immediately the temperature jumps. He brings another, and another, and another, and another, until it must be 120 degrees inside. At a nod from John, the man closes the blanket and we're in darkness, except for the dim white-hot glow of the rocks. Though I can't see my mother, I know she's pleased and determined. John takes a dipper of sage-filled water from the bucket by his side and douses the rocks, which hiss and spit. Steam rises, covers me like a cloak. The first round is in honor of the world's children, and John begins to pray.

I know the sweat will probably be several rounds from ten to forty-five minutes each, depending on John's direction. Each round has a theme, honoring women or children or the treepeople. We could pay tribute to telephone poles for all I care: I'm trying not to lose it. Part of the fear comes from knowing this has just begun, that I might have two more hours and already I'm claustrophobic. I think: *I can't do this. If I don't scream, I'll die—I'll pitch headlong into those rocks.* My mother's words come back to me. "The heat is Grandfather's breath, so welcome it." I clutch my hawk feather and focus on my breathing, take sips of air, try to cool it before it hits my throat. I press a handful of sage to my mouth like a mask. This is what it must be like to drown. Only instead of water it is air that presses in on you, that steals under your clothes and under your eyelids, between your toes and legs. I imagine the air is black, not because of the darkness but because of its density.

It doesn't occur to me to say "All my relations," the code for exit. Such a simple phrase, the words smooth with no hard consonants. But the implications are too much for me, more damaging than that black heat. It would mean admitting to my mother that I'm lacking, unworthy in some fundamental sense. I would disgrace her before these people whom she loves and who have been good to her—to our family—who have at first tolerated and then accepted her. Introducing me that afternoon she had said, with the pride it always surprised me to hear, "This is my daughter."

Her interest in Indian culture was at first just another in a series of fads she'd embraced over the years and brought home to my brother Dace and me like so many stray cats intended to improve our quality of life. I went through the EST training when I was eight. I camped with organic farmers in the southwest when I was ten, and when I was twelve, a man in a red poncho read my palms by the Pacific Ocean and I was glad to know I'd have a long and full life with many husbands.

I was in junior high when she discovered Findhorn, a magical place in Scotland where people lived in harmony and grew tomatoes the size of cantaloupes. Her enthusiasm was still contagious to me then. I was willing to believe in a better place, better than the gray damp of that small Oregon coastal town and its incessant fog, our drafty apartment with the stained linoleum floors, the front yard filled with gravel. Although I believed in these better places, I was vaguely afraid that if she did find her people, I would be unable to follow. I knew she was looking for something and hadn't found it in me.

Eventually she stopped talking about Findhorn and shelved the books, though now and then I'd take one out and look through the pages, as if there were a picture, a passage, something to tell me what made her turn to something else, what made her leave one thing for another. She began researching her genealogy when I was a teenager and learned that Great-Grandma Fox had been kidnapped briefly by the Siletz Indians. My mother earned a master's degree in social work and, by the time I was finishing high school, became a counselor at the Native American Rehabilitation Association in Portland. Her interest was no longer a fad but a career. Still, I felt lost as her daughter. During her first month on the job, she presented me with a leather medicine bag of hawk's feathers, dried sage, and tiny carved rocks, which hung from a necklace so it could be worn close to the heart. I wore it for a day, but as it was the size of a plum, it was too bulky under my shirt and eventually our dog got ahold of it.

My little brother Dace fit in so easily. From his father he inherited sloping brown eyes, and people would say it looked like "he had some Indian in him." But it was his openness, rather than his looks, that helped him make friends. He came to have the same faith my mother did. He told me once, "Their culture is something you can see: the hawk is the messenger of the spirit, the wolf is a brother. Everything has a purpose. I never understood organized religion— I never saw any angels." What my brother and I did agree on was that Indian culture was better than our generic one, in which we celebrated our heritage only once a year at our Swedish family reunion, where we ate traditional dishes under yellow and blue flags, and one of the great-aunts or -uncles would get drunk and make a scene.

All through high school and college, my mother's houses were filled with Indian things—a hawk's wing arced over the mantel, deerskin drums and folded Navajo blankets in the corners. Shelves overflowed with books on Native American legends and histories. Photos of dignified warriors, wise old women with gray braids, and stoic children wrapped in blankets hung on the walls. Even the babies were wise-looking. These were not clichés to me then. I couldn't see past the images of quiet nobility: these people had a depth I believed I could never reach myself.

At the dances and potlucks, I tried to blend in. How I wanted to. Although I was quiet enough and kept my eyes low, I was just too blond, and I never knew quite when to laugh and when to keep still. Signals were exchanged that I couldn't translate. It never occurred to me that, in part, I created the difficulty, but my mother saw that I did. And then at home: *How could you want to be a cheerleader, why do you lock yourself in your room, why do you wear so much lipstick, can't you get along with your stepfather for once?*

What are we? The things others see, what others want to see. But that is not the truth of us. It's easier to hide than to say: here I am, here are my weaknesses and my fears. Where do we find the courage to open our hearts, to show ourselves to another? Over time, the gap between what I was and what my mother wanted me to be stretched so far it had to be apparent to everyone. I wasn't sure it could ever be closed—or if I even wanted it to be.

Between rounds, we don't leave. When the first one ends after about half an hour, as instructed, we shout an Indian phrase in unison and the fire tender, standing outside, throws open the flap. We gulp warm air like the near drowned. I envy the people near the door and the freshest air. In the half-light I look at my mother, hunched over in exhaustion, hair in wet streaks, skin smeared with dirt. She takes deep and controlled breaths like a woman in labor. After a moment she glances at me and strokes the ground. "The dirt will cool you," she whispers. She puts her face down to her knees and looks at me sideways. I read her lips: *It's better down here.* In spite of her exhausted appearance, it's clear she's enjoying this, and I know she expects that I am, too. I smile weakly and hold up my feather.

John waves for fresh rocks. Four more are piled on, and the flap closes. Again, heat and blackness grip us. John starts a song, keeping time on his small drum. My mother sings quietly. After a few verses a man across the rocks begins to cry. He chokes on his sobs. "Our brother is releasing his pain," John tells us. *"Ohwaa!"* everyone chimes in acknowledgment, in support. Someone to my right coughs heavily. "Let it out!" John shouts. *"Ohwaa!"* comes the chorus. I imagine myself crying like them, all the pain and fear pouring out, flowing into the dry desert where it will seep into the earth, but I can't let go. I'm still an outsider, a stranger.

Round two and round three combine in my mind. I begin to sense the most minute temperature changes. The woman next to me gestures. I can't see it, but I feel tiny hot waves of air and pull away. Working my fingers into the dirt, I cool my fingertips and then press them to my cheeks, slide them over my face, my shoulders, again and again. Time to leave this body.

I'm in desert that sweeps away over scrub brush and rock under which sidewinders and lizards lie, searching for shadow. I crawl through rough sand, knees pierced by locust thorns, skin bitten by fire ants. Which way is home?

The flap opens again. I look around and, despite the crying and coughing, see no trace of panic in anyone's eyes.

I know that a sweat like this requires endurance, that my mother and the others have been coming monthly, many for years, building stamina like layers of sediment. Learning to pace breathing and the heartbeat. Like the man who walks over coals before the gasping people who have not seen the scorched soles during weeks of trials. It's all a terrible mistake. My mother thinks I'm stronger than I am. I realize I will do anything to try to prove myself, and I will not reveal my fear that no matter how she pushes and pulls, I may not ever be who she wants me to be.

I keep waiting for something to shift in me. What round is this? Four, five. I think of the secrets of my mother, the secret pain of our family, the legacy of separated women. A scandal caused my great-grandmother Elsa to flee Sweden and come to America; she left four of her six daughters behind with neighbors, with friends—she cooked in hotels twelve hours a day to be able to send for them. Three did follow years later, the fourth never.

My grandmother Viola came after two years: she was six then and clutched her bunk in the dark hold of the ship, listening to whisperings of languages she didn't understand, the moan of wood against wood, the fierce rush of ocean. What happened to her in those two years of separation? She always said she couldn't remember. As a mother she was distant, often frustrated and sometimes hysterical. But what did she know of love? That it is dangerous? What did she teach my mother, who would give me away starting when I was very young—to sisters, friends, for a day or week, for a summer.

When my mother told me about her childhood, she said there wasn't enough love in her house, that she couldn't wait to leave it.

The prayers now are for prison inmates, for their mothers and daughters and sons. For the addicts, the homeless, the forgotten.

Something is being said: we are the lucky ones, the strong. Our prayers help others. There is a strength in togetherness. My breathing shallow, my head low. Then four fingers—smooth as wet bones—rest briefly on my wrist.

"Be strong," the woman beside me whispers.

"Hmm," I answer, grateful. And I want to tell her about the rivers my mother would take us to when we were little, the rocks silky green on the bottom, the water that held me, carried me, so that sometimes I felt I'd become part of it, my hair its weeds, my bones softened. If I could tell her.

It's over, and for a long time my mother and I stay in the cooling lodge while many of the others creep out slowly to rinse and dress for dinner. The sun slips behind the Sierras, chilling the air, and I think of how fast heat leaves the desert. Dirt dries tight on my damp skin. We look at each other, and she reaches for my hand. Her face is raw with emotion and I smile a little, embarrassed as always by sentiment and ceremony. But I know that somehow this is keenly important to her, that she believes we've shared something that has transformed us both and drawn us closer together. With a strange reluctance, I realize she's right. Should I believe in her?

"You did it," she says, grinning, and though I search her face, I see no surprise, only approval. "You can do anything."

Maybe, I think to myself. We crawl out and find the hose, and I rub off the pasty dirt with cool water, laughing with relief and dizziness. I join my mother, both of us wrapped in blankets, to watch the fading light. She tells me I've been invited to a Christmas Eve sweat during my December visit. It won't be so hot, she says. She wants me to be with her, whether I belong or not.

Whenever I move to a new place, she sends me an envelope of sage for me to burn, and she's taught me to carry the smoking ashes to each corner of the house. This encourages the bad spirits to leave, and then, she says, I can call it home.

27

Wired

We take 44 west through stands of ponderosa pine that recede from view like drawn curtains as we pass, revealing sparse herds of cattle feeding on meadow grass. Late-July morning, clear skies. It could be an ordinary weekend drive in the country, some quality father-daughter time. But he's not my father, he's my step-father, my mother's fourth husband. She met him as he was finishing nearly a decade in the Nevada prison system for armed robbery, and for three years they couldn't move to California because he wasn't yet allowed to cross the state line.

But now Steve can go anywhere he wants, and on this day he's searching for telegraph lines that run along the Southern Pacific Railroad tracks. He's going to show me how he used to steal copper wire.

From November through March, he saw good lines as he cleared snow on Lassen County roads, deep in the mountains of northeast California. I thought of him on those frigid cold days, driving that plow, shoving through tunnels of snow piled high as walls, the winter light dive-bar dim. He brought home the minimum wage and handed it to my mother. When he saw those lines, it must have reminded him of the old days when he didn't work for anyone, when he took what he wanted, when he was free.

. . .

We have the road almost to ourselves—in the past several miles, we've seen only three cars. I sit back and he tells me what to look for. A secluded area, not a lot of traffic. Stealing wire is always done at night, of course. If possible, you want a line far enough off the highway to avoid the wash of headlights.

"You don't want to be always jumping off the pole to hide. It just isn't worth it. You no sooner start cutting than here comes a car."

Desert terrain is best. You can see car lights for twenty miles. In the mountain country like this, there's cover, which you want. But you also won't get a lot of warning. If a train comes along, that's trouble.

"They got those big bright lights, and if they see a line's been cut, they'll call it in."

The railroad detectives still keep on the lookout for wire thieves, for the men Steve used to be. For years, until they caught on, the railroads lost millions of dollars in stolen telegraph line, the rolled copper wire that could sometimes fetch seventy cents a pound.

"Back then, we called 'em 'scores.' We'd go off and just search— kind of like what we're doing right now. We'd get maps from the forest service and take three, four days finding a good spot, partying in the meantime. We needed to check out the access roads, and in case you had to split through the woods, you needed a meeting spot. We'd spend the whole day reconnoitering."

He points out power poles, which aren't what we want. We're looking for the shorter telegraph poles that border the tracks. And then I see them. Steve leans forward and nods with satisfaction. Usually quiet, he's animated now—I can tell he's eager to get started.

"See how far it is? Perfect distance from the road. Nice flat terrain—we wouldn't have to pack our gear up a hill." He speeds up the truck. "We'll see if they've got an access road. The wire's heavy, so you need a good road to get your truck along the tracks. One roll can weigh seventy-five pounds, and if you have to hump it far, it can be a lot of work."

I hand him some crackers and cheese, and we eat as we drive along. We pass an RV full of little kids who stare out at us from the back window. Steve waves at them.

"You know, it was a beautiful thing," he says, looking over at me. "It wasn't like knocking over a bank or a supermarket. And there was very little risk for the money."

I nod, keeping my questions in check. I've often interrupted him too soon, thinking he was finished when he was only pausing. Then we see the road at the same time, and I feel a little thrill. How easy it would be. Steve pulls off, the dirt road curling rolls of dust behind us. Minutes later we reach the line.

He switches off the car and the sudden silence is like an expectation, as if an audience were waiting for us to begin. Without a word, he gets out and stretches a bit, takes a deep breath and lets it out with a sigh. When I join him, he's facing the empty tracks that travel in both directions, and I wait to see which way he will go.

For a long time I wouldn't have taken off alone with Steve—not thirty miles into the mountains. He scared me at first, even after they'd married. And as much as I don't want to admit it, sometimes he still does, even after seven years. He's tall and broadly built, and handsome despite a face scarred from the mace left to fester in his eyes overnight in a jail cell. His hair's thinning, but otherwise you wouldn't know he's past fifty. He's strong and he looks it, and when he walks into a room, even other men give him a little extra room.

When my mother introduced me to him, I wasn't surprised. She never liked the dainty, bespectacled type. She was wildly attracted to Steve, five years younger than she, and I thought, *Christ, even in her fifties she's showing no signs of slowing down.* He was exactly the kind of man my mother has always been drawn to—masculine good looks, an air of dangerous mystery and quiet intelligence, a man who carried a weary strength that she could both draw from and replenish.

Still, none of her other men have had Steve's intense perceptiveness. Those dark eyes take you in, all your motives and fears and insincerities. He learned this skill in prison, and it saved his life more than once. It's unnerving to be on the receiving end. I've caught him observing me as I sweet-talk my mother or try to justify yet another change of plans, and it's as if he knows what I'm doing before I do.

Mostly Steve listens, preferring to let others carry the conversation. He loves to read, especially philosophy and natural science. His curiosity is endless, his interest running from irrigation techniques to the JFK conspiracy and the Civil War to mountain climbing. He'll breeze through anything I recommend, and I often send him books and articles I think he'd like. He prefers to spend time with books more than with people, as if trying to inhale all the knowledge he was denied in prison.

Now and then my mother and I will be talking while Steve reads in the other room, and he'll surprise us by barking out a comment, letting us know that on some level he's always listening. Sometimes he'll shock us. During a discussion about farm animals, he informed us that if you want to get rid of a body, you throw it to pigs.

"They'll eat everything, bones and all," he told us, and we just stared.

Once he gets going with his stories, we listen, fascinated, feeling strangely privileged to be given glimpses of a world we've only read about or seen on TV. Yet it often feels too real. Many of the people in his stories are still around. The drug addict who's been shot four times actually does live somewhere in Wyoming, and for all we know, he may show up at the back door one night.

In the beginning I kept my distance, and I had my own kind of fun imagining Steve's life in his bad-ass days. I'd picked up all kinds of information about him—I'm a good listener, too. Steve was a big drinker and a fan of all kinds of drugs. In the seventies, he wore his hair *Mod Squad* curly, and as he says, "Everyone was getting high back then. Man, it was *normal.*" My mom and he have eight marriages between them, and I remember thinking at their small wedding on the Oregon coast in the chilly rec-room hall, *What's the point?*

I decided right off to avoid arguments with Steve, and I don't take sides between him and my mother. In the beginning, for each of us, the other one was just part of the deal. Our relationship has been largely an unspoken one, but over time it's grown from mutual acceptance to genuine fondness. And there's this: no man's ever lasted so long with us.

. . .

"*Hey,* it's been cut. Someone's been here."

Two of the wires dangle to the ground like lost kite strings. It looks like originally there had been five or six lines, but just two are left—and they're cut. Steve walks fast, climbs the short rocky rise to the pole.

"I'll be damned." He bends down to peer at the cut wire, picking one up and turning it over, running his finger down its length. "They couldn't finish the job. Probably some idiot didn't have a set of headphones to tap in to the line, and the railroad figured it out."

He seems satisfied with his theory and continues scouting around the area. He points to the top of the pole.

"See those? Those're insulators. This once had seven strands. Pretty good. If you only have a score with two lines, you've got to go a long way to roll enough."

Steve's job was climbing the poles. He'd shown me his climbing spurs back at the house, old and faded leather, the spikes long as his thumb. The spike easily pierces the pole, sliding in with a soft crunch.

"Climbing's a tough job. Man, you get tired. But we could make some money tonight."

He stands with his hands on his hips and looks down the tracks, surveying the scene like a property buyer.

"I figure four people, eight hours on a line with seven strands, could yield about ten thousand pounds of wire—or a little over five thousand dollars, depending on market price. Damn!"

He glances at me and then back at the tracks.

"Grand theft is all it is, you know; it's not like armed robbery."

I don't know what to say—I feel like a kid stuck in a dangerous game with no rules, but I also don't want to disappoint him.

For years no one talked about Steve's past, at least not in front of me. I'd come home for holidays and hear him and my mother mention someone who'd been "inside," or he'd comment on something about prisons in the news, but it was always a hushed thing, never explained. To me, it seemed impolite to acknowledge his years in prison; it would have been like asking the details of a chronic illness. I knew he preferred to keep it hidden, the same way he chose shirts with sleeves long enough to cover his prison tattoos.

But it was a fine line, and gradually, *not* talking about it seemed to produce more shame for all of us than talking about it. It was the same discomfort I'd feel when walking by a homeless person, the tension between looking and not looking—and the knowledge that looking away would be, in part, an affront to that person's dignity. Whatever he's done, it doesn't matter to me. *You've made my mother happy,* I want to say. She is finally calm. And I have, for the first time since we were with Mac and I was seven years old, what you could call a family.

And I have to face what his past has meant to me. To some friends I've boasted about it as if it were mine, something I've done, something that has made me tougher or more worldly. From others I've hidden it. I used his past to my advantage, never considering what my ambivalence might mean to him.

That summer, when I asked Steve to show me the wire, I wanted him to believe I wasn't afraid of his past. He never even asked me why I wanted to learn. That's his way—he assumes people have their reasons, and I didn't offer any. He knew I'd written about crime. And that could have been all it was, some kind of professional interest; but it was more than that. The life intrigued me, I won't deny that. The idea of bands of thieves hiking into the mountains and desert, hauling out stolen wire—it called up images of the Old West, the romance of outlaws. Not hurting any individual people, nothing violent, but still the chance of danger and risk. It seemed like something I would have liked. Steve and I are more alike than he thinks.

I love my own father, but he doesn't have much left to give. Steve is trying to be a father to me. And he's been a good thief. *Teach me,* I thought.

"You start when it's good and dark, about an hour after sundown, and as soon as you see the sky change, you gotta get things wrapped up. Head for Boise."

He shows me how to tell if the line is copper. On a sunny day, you can see the glint of green from a certain angle. I stand under the last lines and squint into the sun. I can just see it.

"You develop a knack," he says.

If the day is cloudy, you have to climb up and hold a magnet to the wire—copper won't stick; steel will. He looks up at the insulators on the tops of the poles; from the ground they resemble big colored lightbulbs.

"You know, those things are worth two, three dollars apiece. Maybe I'll come back one of these nights—just to have 'em," and he laughs a little to show he's joking.

We walk along the tracks. The day has begun to warm, and the sun falls heavy on us, the way it will at higher elevations. He tells me stories from the past, about Crazy Dennis who'd sip whiskey from a fruit jar all night long. Once lightning struck him while he climbed a pole.

"Knocked him clear to the ground. Went right through him. He had these big sores on the bottoms of his feet, big as plums," Steve says, chuckling.

And there was the time they had the bright idea to get one of those railroad handcarts that travel along the tracks to haul the wire. They'd piled up about two thousand dollars' worth of wire before they heard the distant chug of the train.

"When the train hit it, the cart lit up the sky like a crate full of fireworks. It was like the Fourth of July."

He stops and kicks at the dirt with his boot.

"You had to have money to rent the E-Z Haul, for the motel, food, booze, drugs. A few times we'd get to partying too much, and before we could do the job, we were broke. But mostly we'd finish and then we'd pack the rolls into the truck and take it to a metal-salvaging place in Boise. We'd park a couple of blocks away and go see Carl, one of the owners. They'd dump it right in and cut it up. They paid us cash. *Cash.* Right on the spot. Man, he loved to see us comin'."

He pauses and takes a long drink of water.

"Once he talked about setting us up with a semi, but nothing ever came of that. We were young and wild. Getting the semi would have been too much like a job—then we'd be working for *him.*"

Steve starts along the tracks again, hands in his pockets. It's been almost twenty-five years since he's scouted a line. I don't ask him what I really want to know: I want to know if he'll ever leave, if he'll get tired of the shit jobs and the routine and the bills, the cutesy Christmas dinners, if he'll get tired of people like me wondering— of the look in our eyes. I wonder if one day an old friend will call from Alaska or Montana and offer him some kind of deal. I want to know if he'll leave my mother, leave her for this. She loves him with a conviction I've never seen in her. For once I'm willing to trust that she's settled down. I want to believe that she can.

How do I know he's changed, that he's not the man he was? He's different than before, it's true. But I've seen men leave for less. And I've done my own share of leaving. I know how easy it can be.

We turn back, the only sound the soft crunch of our hiking boots on the dry ground. Then, surprising me, he starts talking as if I'd asked him the question, the question I've never spoken.

"I was a drug runner," he says, and I just listen. "Sometimes I wouldn't have anything going. For me this was always a good backup."

Up ahead the truck sits, dusty and abandoned-looking. I keep quiet while we walk and wait for him to go on.

"When I was young, I loved stealing. There's a freedom to it. You're in business for yourself. It's like you're standing outside society. I loved the thrill. Now, some things, like purse snatching, we'd look down on. But no matter what, I choose not to be a thief today. Armed robberies—I can't even imagine doing that now. When you stick a gun in someone's face, anything can happen. It's repulsive to me now. I don't want to hurt people for money."

I know this is for me, that he wants me to know he's not going back—that he's different now.

We walk back to the truck in silence, and I wonder how we'll end this day, how we'll ever talk about anything else. Suddenly, he scares me, his voice harsh and low from his side of the truck.

"Joelle, come here!"

I join him, and in the distance, maybe a quarter mile to the west,

I see them—a herd of deer galloping. I've never seen so many—three, maybe four dozen, tight together. Then they shift with an instinctive fluidity, veering swiftly in another direction, the way birds, as if connected by wire, will perfectly alter their course. I think something must be hunting them, the way they run and shift, run and shift. But there's nothing else, only the wave of deer. Steve and I watch, stunned into silence.

"Let's try to get closer," Steve says in a whisper, as if the animals could hear us, and we get in the truck and drive slowly along the access road, parallel to the herd and the railroad tracks alongside us. The road takes us no closer, and then the herd is gone. But he's still driving, still looking; I can see the disappointment in his face. He looks out at empty land, and I want to bring him back.

"Were they deer?" I ask.

"No, no way," he says quietly. "They were much too big. They were most likely elk."

I wonder aloud if they could be antelope. Steve lets the car roll to a stop and thinks for a minute, hands still on the wheel. Around us, dust rises and settles in the quiet heat.

"They had to be elk, because elk are basically one shade of brown. Antelope, now—antelope have contrasting colors, and they move more gracefully, too. That's how you know."

And he looks over at me then, as if to make sure I understand the difference.

28

Notes from Maui

I was thirty-three, living in a nowhere town in northern California, when a postcard came in the mail from Maui from Ken's
mother. *Your father is very sick. His liver. You should call.*

It was September, and the heat was stifling. I stood in the driveway while trucks sped by, showering me with dust, and read it again
and again. *This is how is begins,* I thought. I had been waiting for this
for years—a phone call or a letter about my father. Everyone knew
he'd die young from the drinking, the smoking. For years, whenever visiting, I'd hear him coughing in the morning, the sound so
brutal and strangling I'd have to go outside to escape it. I thought I'd
prepared myself, that one day, when he began to die, I'd be ready.
But instead I was astonished—and for the next few months I lived
each day in a state of numb disbelief.

I was teaching and had to finish out the semester, and by then the
concern over the millennium, Y2K, and terrorism only increased
my dread of what was happening to my father. He was diagnosed
with cirrhosis of the liver, and was living on Maui with my brother
Ken. By the time I got there, Dad was basically bedridden. The only
people he would see were me and Ken, Ken's wife and child, and
our friends. The look on his own friends' faces offended and embarrassed him. He didn't blame them for their reaction; he didn't

recognize himself, either. Each time he looked in the mirror, it took a while to recover from the shock. The cirrhosis had caused the tissue under his skin to recede, with only the bones remaining to give the face meaning. He had become eerily youthful, the skin smooth and soft again. I wondered what was worse for him—the physical suffering or the indignity. He'd always loathed doctors and any display of weakness.

Although I was scared the first time I saw him, after a while the familiar mannerisms reassured me—the way he'd shake his head slowly when he was annoyed, pressing his lips together, was a gesture I'd seen hundreds of times. There was still his thick shock of gold hair, so full I imagine a stranger might think it a wig; and most of all there were his green eyes, all the more prominent, wide open as if to see all that he could. Traces of his humor showed from time to time, and so did his kindness—he was worried that I wasn't comfortable, sleeping out on the couch.

Every evening I sat while my brother massaged our father's shoulders and rubbed lotion into his parched skin. I was surprised and moved by this nightly ritual. The TV always played, and the three of us watched—a game show or the news (on New Year's Eve, we watched the celebrations as they traveled the globe toward us). We were a strange audience, the TV providing a small check on the intimacy of the moment: my brother massaging our father, the paraphernalia of illness around us (baskets of medicine; the walker at the end of the bed). But there was a wonderful peacefulness at those times.

Halfway through my visit, my brother and I took our father to the hospital. His swollen belly had made it almost impossible for him to sleep, even with sedatives, and he could hardly move—his lungs were crowded, pressed by the toxic fluid his liver couldn't process anymore. He would need to have the fluid drained, a gruesome, excruciating process. He'd been through it once before, and he was scared. We helped him to the car. It was the first time he'd been outside since his last doctor's appointment weeks before, and though he dreaded the hospital, he said, "It's nice out today," as if everything were normal, and I knew he did it for our benefit. As Ken drove, I watched him, the enormity of what he had been through these past months only starting to become clear. I thought of how, when he was just seven, he used to put blankets over our father and tuck them in around his shoulders.

At the hospital, feeling utterly useless, I tried to keep busy. I adjusted the pillow behind my father's back; wrapped a blanket around his feet (he was always cold); read newspaper articles that he didn't want to hear. At some point I realized he let me do this because he knew I needed to. He told me I was a "frustrated nurse." I scowled at anyone who stared as I pushed him in the wheelchair. I would have swum to the next island if he wanted fresh papayas. My fierceness surprised me; I wondered if this was what it would be like if I had a child. The waiting was endless, awful, and through it all, the three of us seemed so exposed—we had to wait in the middle of the bustle of the nurse's station, our father shrunken in his wheelchair, my brother and I on each side.

During the paracentesis, my brother and I watched as six liters of fluid were drained from our father's abdomen. Our father winced and shut his eyes, his body rigid, but he kept silent through it. Once the tube fell out and had to be reinserted, but not before fluid leaked everywhere. I gripped his thin shoulder, whispering, *"It's okay, it's almost over, you have nice new sheets waiting for you on your bed."* As if that made any difference. The bottles of fluid were filled one by one, lined up on the floor, and I fought back nausea and tears, the urge to scream. Because my father's case was so advanced, this procedure was essentially useless, would help only briefly, giving him a reprieve for a couple of weeks. It was too late to do anything else to save him.

The clock said twenty-four minutes had passed, but that couldn't be right—it took much longer, there was no measuring. And it took part of my life.

At some point in each day, there's nothing left to be done. No food or medicine, no music, not even words. You are reduced to your own love. That's all you have left to give. It's a feeling of being stripped to the core. In its intensity, it most closely resembles passionate love, because both the lover and the child are afraid they won't survive the loss. Yet this love is even more pure; there is no room for resentment, no selfish worry that he will leave me for another.

Nothing had prepared me, not even my grandfather's death two months before. My grandfather was eighty-eight and tired. My father was not even sixty. I thought, *I'm not ready to do this.*

For days my brother gathered Roman candles, smoke bombs, firecrackers, and sparklers for our own millennium celebration. Fireworks are legal in Hawaii, and the papers were full of safety precautions. My brother arranged the packages like presents in front of the Christmas tree and, like a child, continually picked them up and felt their weight. He had the same love of holidays that our father always had. It didn't matter which one; even for Saint Patrick's Day, Dad would call for corned beef and beer and wear a bit of green on his clothing—and we weren't even Irish.

Almost every other family, for blocks and blocks of the Kahului neighborhood, had their own private celebrations as well, and from sunset on, we heard people cheering and the whistles and crackle of fireworks. By ten the air hung heavy with smoke that traveled thick as coastal fog down our street. Our town resembled a war zone, with rockets and smoke bombs and the rattle of random firecrackers. We kept checking on our father, who would normally be asleep by then. I told myself, *He's all right, he's all right.*

Because he couldn't make it to the front yard, a little before midnight we set up a row of fireworks so he could see from his window. We helped him to get up, waiting until the last minute so he wouldn't have to stand long. Through the smoke, the palm trees looked like giant gray flowers towering above us. My brother's friend lit the fireworks, which ignited with a fierce *hiss,* bright reds and greens and blues reaching for the heavens, lighting the world and all of us in it. I looked up at my smiling father, and his face was glowing, glowing and alive.

·   ·   ·

I left Maui soon after to go back to work; I was broke, my rent was due, and my brother's house was crowded. I could have stayed, of course, could have found a way. But I was weak, and afraid, and also I was angry and confused. He was still in his fifties; he would never see me have a child. None of it made sense, and I couldn't face it anymore. And what I wouldn't admit to anyone: there was someone waiting for me back in California, someone who would hold me through the nights. So I left my brother to care for our father until the end, and I will have to live with that.

I kept in contact with my father by phone, but I never saw him again. He died five weeks later, and I got back to Maui the next day, too late. That week we flew to Oahu and scattered his ashes and plumeria flowers in the same bay that held his father's and mother's ashes.

Over the next year I kept thinking about the photo collage that hung on the wall of the room where he was dying those last months of 1999. I remember sitting in the armchair across from his bed, where you could look from what he had been, in the pictures, to what he had become. The collage was a present from his ex-wife Suzi. There's his high school portrait, his father at a typewriter, another of his parents and brother in front of a ship, covered in leis. I'm there in one of the small center ovals, a shot taken maybe twenty years ago, wearing a smile and a yellow cardigan that I've wrapped tightly around me, as if I'm cold—but there is the smile. My brother at eight or nine, smiling, too, in his own oval.

The first time I saw the collage, it startled me to see my picture there, even though I'm his only daughter. Why wouldn't my picture be included? But I was surprised for a reason. I've never felt like someone inside my father's world. I know there were huge silences between us, that we just skated over the surface of a deep well of feeling. We never had the tearful bedside confession. I never told him how sorry I was for my cowardice, for the thousands of times I said nothing, for the times I ordered a beer when I should have said, "We both know you'll die if you don't stop drinking. I'll take you to an A.A. meeting, whatever you need. Let me help you."

I was just like him—terrified of any kind of confrontation. We both hated emotional outbursts and strictly avoided them. There was an unspoken agreement: that at least with each other we were safe, from what I'm still not sure. From the truth, maybe. With my father the boundaries were clear, and the price we paid was that we never really knew each other.

Not long ago I picked up my father's novel, which I've carried with me since 1983, the year it was published. I hadn't really looked at it since I read it at seventeen. On the cover, his name is very small, but the title, *Gone to Maui,* is large and dramatic. The book jacket warns that it's "the book the developers tried to ban." There's no picture of him. When I open the first pages, I see my name: he dedicated the book to my brother Ken and me. *Gone to Maui* did well in Hawaii, had kind of a cult following for a while. My brother even used the novel in his English classes at the high school because it's one of the few books the local kids can relate to. They like the pidgin English, the references to local foods and geography—and especially the theme of respect for the *aina,* the land. I felt the weight of the book in my hands. This book is all that Ken and I have left of our father. That and each other.

I started to read it one Sunday morning, a little over a year after my father died, and it was still light when I finished. It was a good story, one I would have liked no matter who wrote it. I read parts of it aloud, as if to hear his voice. Sometimes I laughed hard—we'd always shared the same humor. I came across familiar phrases of his: "Hey you old fox!" And certain stories I'd heard him tell many times, like his funny yet accurate take on the differences among Hawaii's different ethnic groups. The poked fun aimed at haoles—at himself. The regret for the way Hawaii was being paved over.

There's a passage about leaving Maui, how the plane banks over the entire island and you can see all of it spread out below you like a map—very close, only a few hundred feet below, beautiful and green and clear. I love it because I could have written it myself: *There was something about leaving Maui. Something emotional that had to do with the flight pattern. You could look down and think, There. There, I did this. There, that happened. You couldn't do that anywhere else. But leav-*

*ing Kahului airport you could see the exact street where you parked your car
before a party. You could see where you'd worked, gotten sick, made love.*

As I read, I started to get nervous. Many of the characters were
drinkers and gamblers and womanizers. I began to see aspects of
him in nearly every person, even the women, as if the book's characters were merely reflected sides of the prism of my father's personality. Still, they remained elusive, like rumors. So I kept reading,
looking: looking for him. I came across passages that seemed to be
answers to questions I'd never asked, and then they'd just as quickly
slip away. Here's one in which he appears to explain his mistakes—
but it soon widens to be a sort of cultural apology for a generation:

*That seemed to be my story on Maui. I couldn't get it right. I ebbed when
flowing was obvious. I flowed when everyone else was ebbing so hard they
were about to fall off the face of the earth. I just couldn't get it right. I wasn't
alone, though. In one way or another everyone I knew was going downhill. I
think it was the pursuit of pleasure. It got to us all. Somewhere around 1970
we looked around and decided we'd had enough with causes and protest. We
were here on earth to be pleased. Think about it. What pleases you? Do you
pursue it?*

Yes, I do, I said to myself as I read the words. I kept on, trying to
learn more about him. I knew this was selfish, the quotes pulled un-
fairly out of context, but I couldn't stop myself—I was using the
book as a way to connect with him, a book he wrote twenty-five
years ago. A conversation with a man who was gone. I still had so
many questions: What was so enticing about gambling? Did he have
any regrets? How did he really feel about women? I suppose I
hoped he might be candid in the book, his true views exposed
through his characters. Often I didn't like what I found. One of the
main characters, Bryan, is a gambling addict, and he gets in the kind
of trouble my father used to at one time—the deep kind, syndicate-
level, where mean burly men visit you if you're not careful.

Here's Bryan, owing so much money his life is in danger, delud-
ing himself: *He'd watch the players. It was slower that way but he knew it
was safer. Sooner or later the hot hand would show, and he'd be there. He'd
ride it and win, and then he'd tip everyone in sight.* My father hadn't done
library research for this book; he'd lived it. He called it "action"—

the kind of action that came from point spreads and dice bouncing across green felt.

I got tense whenever the male characters reflected about women. Here's what one character thought about his wife:

There were times when he still loved Bonnie, but never when she was awake or near him. The only thing Bonnie had become for him was necessary. He understood this and was comfortable with it. There had never been a woman in his life who was anything else.

People had told me my father had used women. One of his wives said to me, "Your father chose women who kept it together." It was true: all three of his wives were dynamic, strong women. But I knew my father had loved the women in his life, even if he was attracted to their strength. And this *was* a work of fiction. But I ignored my better judgment. As I kept reading, I found to my relief (and chagrin) that most of the female characters were complex, intelligent people, wholly sympathetic.

In the end, the narrator dies of an illness after a stay in the hospital, the words so eerily premonitory of my father's own eventual, horrible death: *I'm scared. For the first time, I'm truly scared. . . . [W]hen the doctors come they wear masks. . . . Something's wrong, and now I know why I keep writing this. I'm talking about maybe the last things I did.*

Of course, reading the book didn't really bring me any closer to my father. He'll always be elusive, always be a part of me that's missing. Every time I read a book or write a story, I'll want to tell my father about it. He still had things to teach me, and that loss is an ache that never lessens. So I keep his book with me because it's all I have, and because one of the lines still follows me, won't let me go. I can even hear him say it, as if it was a question he would ask himself sometimes, and I wonder if he ever got an answer, and if not knowing kept him drinking. It's in the prologue. The narrator, unnamed until the end, teases us with this mystery: *I'm one of the characters—maybe good, maybe bad. I don't know yet.*

But I do. I wish I could tell him.

29

Where Love Is

M y mother and I meet in San Francisco for the weekend. A friend has let us stay at her apartment, and our plan is to visit museums and bookstores and try out some good restaurants, since we both live in such small towns. On Saturday morning we consider our choices, which overwhelm us. How can we fit it all in? There is so little time, and I begin to feel anxious. How can we see the modern art museum and the Georgia O'Keeffe exhibit, on opposite sides of the city, and still do what she wants (the garden show at the Cow Palace) and what I want (go see the new film *Boys Don't Cry*)? What about the walk to breakfast at that cute place on Lombard? The bookstore on Chestnut? And then blues at John Lee Hooker's place that evening . . .

We rule out the garden show (which takes us out of the city) and the film (why sit indoors for two hours), and as I follow her out the door, I try to resist the thought: *Is this real, does she really enjoy it— being with me?* But the day falls into place, breakfast and the walk, and we don't get lost, as we thought we might. It's been so long since we've been in San Francisco together—and we discover that there are so many neighborhoods, so many parts of the city, we've never seen.

I have a great time with her—there's a lot of laughter and conversation, and she surprises me with a photography book at the museum store, and it occurs to me again how well we get along. By the time we get to the Legion of Honor, the O'Keeffe exhibit is closing, but we can still see our favorite pictures beyond the rope, only a few feet away, and side by side we look at them, and that is good enough, absolutely.

Back at the apartment, we make some tea and talk about our fathers, who died within four months of each other. We both feel unmoored somehow. Neither of us had understood their mysterious worlds, had been invited in for only brief, intriguing glimpses. She and I held out, always, for yet more proof that they loved us. We talked about how long it took to realize that our fathers did love us, more than we imagined, whether they always showed it or not. How ironic, that at nearly the same time we both lost the most important men in our lives, the ones against whom all others must compare.

Later, as we get dressed for dinner, I offer to do my mother's makeup. She never did know how to do it right—for her, it was always an afterthought. I carefully brush the tips of her eyelashes with a mascara brush. Unlike me, she has such fine, tiny lashes, such sparse eyebrows. In so many small ways we are different, yet we're told all the time that we look alike. It's the Swedish bone structure, people say. For a few years now, my mother's been flattered to be compared to me, but I'm not prettier than she is, just younger.

She loves it when I make up her face, which I do about once a year for special occasions. I realize as I lean in to apply the eyeliner and feel her breath on my arm that this is the closest I ever get to her, aside from the brief, obligatory hugs we give when we first see each other and when we leave. It's me who keeps the distance, though, not her. Even when I feel close to her—as I have so many times today—I don't reach out. If I were another kind of daughter, I would have. I would have hugged her, told her I loved her. But though it shames me, I wasn't able to. And I can't help stiffening when she reaches for me, even though I know it's out of love. Memories live within my body, written so long ago on the flesh and bones: the years of fighting and crying, the times she's lashed out at me in rage. And yet I'm drawn to her still. I envy other mothers and daughters who can touch so comfortably, who rest arms on each other's shoulders or hold hands. Words and memories fade, though, if you let them. I won't rush this trust, it's delicate and precious.

Before we leave for dinner, she calls Steve, and from across the room I watch out of the corner of my eye. It's such a familiar image from my past, my mother on the phone, preoccupied, off limits. But she's happy, relaxed, telling Steve about our day: the William Gedney photographs of the sixties at the Museum of Modern Art, the Rodin sculpture at the Legion of Honor. He says something and she laughs: he's teasing her, I can tell. They've been married almost ten years.

I used to resent these distractions, to be threatened by them. I knew that she was okay only if the man in her life was okay. Her priorities were clear to me. I would think: *Don't you see? Men come and go—I'm your daughter, and I'll never leave.* But it's different now. I believe she and Steve will be together for the rest of their lives, and she no longer has to choose between the man and her child. I don't need her to anymore. She can love us both.

What I've come to understand is this: I have two mothers, the one from the past and the one today. Both live on; the one from childhood doesn't notice me, and again I return to another fixed image. I'm maybe seven or eight, standing in the door quietly, and inside the room my mother is distracted. I wait, hoping to get her attention, but she waves me away, impatient, upset. It is up to me to let this image go, to forgive. She's hung up the phone and is looking at me now and smiling, this woman, the mother of today. I realize she's been here for me for a pretty long time.

Before we leave, she asks me if I wouldn't mind putting a towel over the liquor that sits on a tray in the living room. There's Scotch, bourbon, gin—all gleaming in their crystal decanters like something on a movie set.

"I really don't want to look at it," she says, and pauses before looking at me. "I used to like bourbon, you know."

And for a minute my father's absence is just as real to me as my mother's presence, as she sits on the couch in her green sweater. I think of how, because she got sober when I was fourteen, my mother and I never drank together the way I did with my father. I suddenly feel a rush of gratitude for A.A., for my father telling her to go even after he gave it up. It's as if I've just realized there was a close call, some bullet missed, and that it is an amazing gift that my mother is still with me. I've taken so much for granted. Have I ever really known about what she has had to overcome? I say a silent thank-you for her strength and cover the bottles, but no matter how I drape the towel, their shapes can still be seen.

The next day, at a coffee shop on Fillmore, I suggest a writing exercise, because she also loves to write, though she never has time. The idea is to choose a word and write for ten minutes, letting the mind wander around memories and associations. She lets me pick, so I choose *light*. We write steadily, but now and then I look up at her, and I can see how hard she's trying. After ten minutes, we read what we've come up with. She's written a lovely passage about a dream she once had. I read my page, about the light on the Oregon coast, the way I remember it from twenty years ago.

"The mist and the dimness, it was always dim, wasn't it?" I say. And for a moment those years are between us, cold and damp and impassable. She agrees, then she smiles.

"But do you remember the beach in August and September, how warm it could be, how the sun would come out and it was incredible?"

I think of the crystalline days when we didn't need to wear coats, when my mother and brother and I could walk barefoot on the sand together. Those days, rare and perfect.

As we walk to the marina the last morning, she tells me about a painful memory from a Christmas vacation when I was home from the University of Hawaii, visiting her in Mill Valley. We hadn't seen each other since the previous May. My brother Dace was home, too, and we had plans to trim the tree. Dace and I had made cookies, and apple cider simmered on the stove. We looked forward to this ritual, one of our favorite things to do together. There was the unspoken feeling that through all the changes, through all the fathers, these ceremonies helped keep us together. Even if we were in a new house, a new town, each December we hung the same felt candy canes, the same gold balls, the thread unraveling over the years.

But our mother was upset—Brad had recently moved out and they were headed for divorce. It was the end of another marriage, the departure of another man, and it hadn't gotten easier over time; if anything, it was harder. She had less of herself to lose.

"Brad called and we had this terrible argument on the phone—and I had to leave to see him in person," she tells me now as we walk. "There was no question. I was frantic. I told you and Dace to wait for me, that I'd be back in time because you both had plans later that night. Deep down, though I didn't want to admit it, I knew I couldn't make it back—the drive would take forty-five minutes to San Rafael at that time of day. But all I could think about was seeing Brad.

"When I got there, he wasn't even home. He'd left. And I drove back like a madwoman because it dawned on me that this was probably the last time the three of us would do the tree together, just the three of us, before you were all grown up. This was the last year that I could still call you a kid. I was so afraid that I would miss it, and I thought of all the things I've missed—and for what?"

I imagine her, speeding down 101, crying, pulled in all the directions of her life—the feeling of being torn apart: she parks and runs in the house, calling for us, but we've left, gone off with friends. She walks in and sees the tree, decorated with the ornaments we've had since childhood, looped with colored lights. It's beautiful. I can see her there, sitting with the tree, alone.

We walk for a while in silence, and the bay lies before us at the bottom of the hill and beyond: Sausalito, where she carried me on those mornings after the fog lifted, the places we foraged for clothes and flowers; and Mill Valley, where that last Christmas passed so long ago. She starts walking more slowly, her arms crossed tightly across her chest, but she's calm.

"I'm sorry," she says.

And I tell her it's all right, because it is, and because I'm sorry, too. It's all right because I finally understand her. The same emptiness in her also lives in me. We're so alike, my mother and I. My needs and fears are just a variation of hers. It was she who introduced me to the territory of men, after all, the place where we have looked for love outside of ourselves.

At the marina, in silent agreement, we start along the walkway with the wind at our backs. The city's bright buildings cover the hills on our left, and ahead, the Golden Gate Bridge spans the bay in one long arc, the water below a calm blue in the morning sun. It feels like a brand-new place, as if I've never been here before—or not for a very long time. She takes my hand, and together we walk toward it.